INSPECT BEFORE YOU BUY

Insider Secrets You Need to Know About Home
Inspection — With Companion CD-ROM

Charlie Rose

INSPECT BEFORE YOU BUY
INSIDER SECRETS YOU NEED TO KNOW ABOUT HOME INSPECTION —
WITH COMPANION CD-ROM

Copyright © 2007 by Atlantic Publishing Group, Inc.
1401 SW 6th Ave • Ocala, Florida 34471 • 800-814-1132 • 352-622-1875–Fax
Web site: www.atlantic-pub.com • E-mail: sales@atlantic-pub.com
SAN Number: 268-1250

ISBN-13: 978-1-60138-031-9   ISBN-10: 1-60138-031-3

Library of Congress Cataloging-in-Publication Data
Rose, Charles Arnold, 1973-
Inspect before you buy : insider secrets you need to know about home inspection : with CD-ROM / by Charles Arnold Rose.
    p. cm.
 Includes bibliographical references and index.
 ISBN-13: 978-1-60138-031-9 (alk. paper)
 ISBN-10: 1-60138-031-3 (alk. paper)
 1. Dwellings--Inspection. I. Title.

TH4817.5.R67 2007
643'.12--dc22
            2007027794

INTERIOR LAYOUT DESIGN: Vickie Taylor • vtaylor@atlantic-pub.com
PROOFREADER: Angela C. Adams • aadams@atlantic-pub.com

Printed in the United States

Printed on Recycled Paper

We recently lost our beloved pet "Bear," who was not only our best and dearest friend but also the "Vice President of Sunshine" here at Atlantic Publishing. He did not receive a salary but worked tirelessly 24 hours a day to please his parents. Bear was a rescue dog that turned around and showered myself, my wife Sherri, his grandparents Jean, Bob and Nancy and every person and animal he met (maybe not rabbits) with friendship and love. He made a lot of people smile every day.

We wanted you to know that a portion of the profits of this book will be donated to The Humane Society of the United States.

–Douglas & Sherri Brown

THE HUMANE SOCIETY
OF THE UNITED STATES ©

The human-animal bond is as old as human history. We cherish our animal companions for their unconditional affection and acceptance. We feel a thrill when we glimpse wild creatures in their natural habitat or in our own backyard.

Unfortunately, the human-animal bond has at times been weakened. Humans have exploited some animal species to the point of extinction.

The Humane Society of the United States makes a difference in the lives of animals here at home and worldwide. The HSUS is dedicated to creating a world where our relationship with animals is guided by compassion. We seek a truly humane society in which animals are respected for their intrinsic value, and where the human-animal bond is strong.

Want to help animals? We have plenty of suggestions. Adopt a pet from a local shelter, join The Humane Society and be a part of our work to help companion animals and wildlife. You will be funding our educational, legislative, investigative and outreach projects in the U.S. and across the globe.

Or perhaps you'd like to make a memorial donation in honor of a pet, friend or relative? You can through our Kindred Spirits program. And if you'd like to contribute in a more structured way, our Planned Giving Office has suggestions about estate planning, annuities, and even gifts of stock that avoid capital gains taxes.

Maybe you have land that you would like to preserve as a lasting habitat for wildlife. Our Wildlife Land Trust can help you. Perhaps the land you want to share is a backyard—that's enough. Our Urban Wildlife Sanctuary Program will show you how to create a habitat for your wild neighbors.

So you see, it's easy to help animals. And The HSUS is here to help.

The Humane Society of the United States
2100 L Street NW
Washington, DC 20037
202-452-1100
www.hsus.org

CONTENTS

——

FOREWORD

by Ken Lambert

The most important aspect of buying any new home is not getting the lowest mortgage rate, getting the biggest house you can afford, or getting that newly constructed house with the granite counters and stainless steel appliances.

Yes, that front yard with the perfect landscaping and stone paver walkway might be nice, but the most important part of buying a new home is understanding what you are getting for your money and, more importantly, what you might be getting yourself into. The one clear way to accomplish this is via a thorough and professional home inspection. This handbook lists some key information regarding choosing your home inspector, but also contains a wealth of practical information for any homeowner well after they have signed on the dotted line.

This book is laid out in a straightforward manner, which allows the reader to walk through a property in much the same manner as a professional. It is in this way that nothing is forgotten or overlooked. Watch your inspector carefully. He should have a "plan" and a checklist. If he looks like he is just trying to take up two hours, maybe you should have been more careful when you checked his references and qualifications. One note I would like to make is that, when it comes to something as critical as a home inspection, please do not hire the cheapest inspector in the telephone book or local newspaper. As with most things in life, you do get what you pay for. It is well worth an additional $150 (or so) if it saves you significant money and aggravation later on — years after you move in.

But this book is far more than something that should be glanced through only during your house-hunting venture. I believe it will be a valuable resource during your tenure in your new home. One thing I have learned after living in and building dozens and dozens of homes (no matter what the house age) is that "it's always something!" Homeowners who seek guidance from this book will be much better equipped to handle the myriad of minor emergencies and inconveniences that come with owning property.

You have made a wise investment by purchasing this inspection handbook, and it will make you a more astute home buyer.

Good luck with your search, and do not forget to keep this edition somewhere nearby — as I am certain you will reach for it again and again.

Ken Lambert has worked extensively in the following areas of real estate in Massachusetts and New Hampshire: real estate development, property inspections, construction estimating, project managing, site supervision, construction financing, as well as mortgage sales.

Contact Information
Web site: **http://homequitybuilder.mortgagefit.com**
E-mail: amfinfo@comcast.net
Phone: 978-764-8470

House Inspection Tip #1

Check the stairs to see if there are any loose boards or nails
that may stick up. Climb them to make sure they are sturdy and
to see if they squeak.

INTRODUCTION

Imagine buying a home, getting everything moved in, and then settling down for a nice quiet evening. Everything seems perfect until you notice a small hole in the wall in the living room. You walk through the kitchen and notice the floor around the refrigerator is soft. You turn on the dishwasher while watching television, and you lose electricity in two rooms of the house. As you stand surrounded by darkness, you hear something scurrying across the floor.

You just spent 10 times more money on this house than you have ever spent on anything. What did you get for all that money? What have you done? More important, what are you going to do? If only you had inspected your home before actually signing on the dotted line.

While this exact scenario is a bit far-fetched, it is not uncommon to find problems with a home after you move in if you did not take the time to inspect the home beforehand or spend the money to have someone else inspect it for you.

If it is in a home, we have done our best to cover it in this book.

This book will teach you what you need to know to inspect any house whether you are buying, selling, or professionally inspecting homes. It will discuss everything from the basement to the roof and even the property around the house. You will learn about electricity, plumbing, landscaping, and repairs. The overriding caution is to avoid homes with structural damage unless you intend to invest a great deal of money and time.

This book will take you through the house systematically in a logical and easy to understand fashion. The table of contents, along with the chapter heading and sub-headings, will help you find any topic quickly and easily.

With this book as your inspecting companion, you will be able to buy and move into your new home with every confidence that you have made a great purchase. If you are selling a house, it will help you identify problem areas that need your attention, and if you are a real estate agent, you can use this book to be aware of possible problems to save yourself legal repercussions from a sale. Not only do we tell you what to inspect and how to inspect it, the book goes into detail about how things work so that you will have the necessary knowledge and background when performing your inspection.

While you may be required to hire a certified home inspector, you can narrow the field among the houses you are considering by either eliminating those where you find serious problems or by preparing to negotiate down the price before calling in a professional to confirm your suspicions. In some states, home inspectors are not permitted to lift, move, or detach anything even if they suspect a problem. In some states, real estate agents are allowed to recommend home inspectors (their friends), and both parties expect to profit from the inspection. Massachusetts has outlawed such collusion but it still goes on, as one home inspector reports:

CASE STUDY: MICHAEL QUINN

Sometimes it seems that the more detailed one is on an inspection, and the more detailed your report, the less endearing you are to the (real estate) agents. I have always enjoyed doing inspections for sellers prior to the sale. This is where this business will  ultimately best serve the consumer. Disclose everything, and price the house accordingly. Empower the seller to do repairs if they want, or just disclose it and get a quote in case it is needed.

US INSPECT
PROFESSIONAL HOME INSPECTIONS

Michael Quinn
Area Manager

America's Leading Home Inspection Company

90 Foxbourne Road
Penfield, NY 14526

Phone: (585) 381-6370
mquinn@usinspect.com

House Inspection Tip #2

Check to see if the fireplace damper opens and shuts easily. Make note if there are any cracks or gaps in the fireplace structure. See if there is a spark-arrester screen. Also make sure to check the chimney to see if it is in good condition.

1

SERIOUS CONCERNS

Inspecting for poisons and carcinogens may make the difference between life and death. This chapter will discuss asbestos, lead poisoning, radon testing, carbon monoxide testing, water quality, and fuel tanks.

ASBESTOS

Asbestos is a concern for people because it is known to cause cancer, usually of the lungs after its fibers have been inhaled. When its fibers mix with a binding agent, they can be used in vinyl floor tiles, cement siding, roof shingles, ceiling tiles, blown-in insulation, flexible fabric connections in duct work, textured paints, textured coatings, spackling compounds, boiler insulation, pipe insulation, putties, caulk, and many other products. The actual asbestos content varies from as low as 1 percent to as much as 75 percent.

Remember that the presence of asbestos in the house does not automatically mean that there is danger. As long as the asbestos does not break apart and become airborne, it is no problem. If you see asbestos in an area where it cannot be damaged, is not deteriorating, nor posing a threat of the fibers becoming airborne, the Environmental Protection Agency (EPA) recommends simply leaving it alone.

Almost all the materials that once contained asbestos are no longer made; however, it may have been used in any houses built before 1978. Removal of the asbestos is usually not recommended because removal releases fiber in to the air, and that is exactly when it is most hazardous. Any asbestos released must be contained and taken away to a designated asbestos landfill. Contact a certified trained professional who deals with asbestos whenever it must be removed. Be aware that it is a dangerous substance. The EPA has a list of past and present uses for asbestos which may be helpful for knowing where to look when checking for signs of asbestos in a house. The site is also useful for knowing what to do if you do see asbestos as well as other pertinent information for a potential homeowner. See their site at **http://www.epa.gov/asbestos/pubs/ashome. html#Home**.

Often it is difficult to know whether asbestos is present, but a common place is in the lining on heating pipes. It looks like corrugated cardboard from the ends. If you find it, check for crushed, torn, or loose sections.

LEAD POISONING

Lead poisoning is considered the number one environmental threat to children. Too much lead in a child's body can cause brain damage and even death. Lower levels of lead in a child's body can cause learning disorders, hyperactivity, and an overall inability to perform well in school. The government estimates that about one of every nine children under six has enough lead in his/her system to pose a problem, that about two-thirds of the homes built before 1940 contain lead paint, and about half of the homes built between 1940 and 1960 contain it. That percentage gets smaller in houses built from 1960 to 1978 when the amount of lead in paint was regulated.

The common misconception with lead paint is that children can be poisoned only by ingesting paint chips, but that is not the only way. Lead is actually in the dust from crumbling lead-based paint. So, if a window sill is painted with lead-based paint, all the child has to do is touch the sill and transfer the any paint dust into his/her mouth for the lead to be taken internally. It can also be delivered in public water in unregulated areas of the country.

Tests are on the market that you can buy to check to see if there is lead in the home. They are easy to use. If you find lead, you should get the help of a professional who knows about lead in the home. Do not try to remove lead paint yourself. The removal must be done by professionals who will control the release of the lead dust and particles and dispose of all the lead paint properly. Greedy landlords are usually reluctant to go to the expense of removing lead paint.

For more information about lead, available from the EPA, visit **http://www.epa.gov/lead/**.

RADON TESTING

Radon is produced by decaying uranium deposits in the ground. It is present in the ground and the atmosphere and is a threat to people when a house is above radon concentrations. It is tasteless, colorless, and odorless. Being exposed to radon for long periods of time can result in cancer, primarily lung cancer.

Houses that are adjacent can have different levels of radon. The amount depends on three factors:

- the amount of uranium-radium in the soil

- the geological formation below the house

- the construction of the home

Obviously, well insulated homes with cracked basement walls will be more at risk for high concentrations of radon because the radon can leak into the home through the cracks.

The amount of radon in a house on a given day will also be affected by rain, snow, wind, barometric pressure, and the use of exhaust fans, fireplaces, and heating systems in the house. Therefore, the only true way of finding a radon problem is to conduct the test over an extended period of time. You may use a commonly available handheld radon tester.

Check with the local health department about whether there is a problem with radon in the well water in the area — a rare occurrence, but something you should definitely consider when looking at purchasing a home with well water.

If you discover radon concentrations, you will need to hire a professional who knows how to correct the problem and alleviate it. Usually it is not a deal breaker for the sale of the home.

For additional information on radon, visit **http://www.epa.gov/radon/** or **http://www.radon.com/**.

CARBON MONOXIDE AND CARBON DIOXIDE TESTING

Unlike other health risks, carbon monoxide (CO) and Carbon Dioxide (CO_2) can kill immediately with no warning — they are invisible and only CO_2 has a taste, which is slightly sour.

Common sources of both are found in every home emanating from anything that uses fossil fuels. Though CO detectors installed in homes can save lives, they do not go off until the CO level reaches a life-threatening level. Therefore, it is a good idea to test the air in the home for traces of CO and CO_2 with a handheld device commonly available for each purpose. If you find trace amounts of either, have a specialist recommend ways to stop the problem before it reaches a dangerous level.

WATER QUALITY

Where you live determines how your water tastes by what is in it. You need only be concerned with your water if you have well water, unless your public water contains lead. You may also want to have your water tested for chloroform. If a well or underground spring provides your water, the water should be tested for a variety of contaminates. It is not the job of the home inspector to test the water. It should be sent to a lab for testing along with specific request for thorough testing. For more information on water quality and water contaminants, visit **http://www.epa.gov/ebtpages/water.html**.

FUEL TANKS

Obviously every home needs a source of heat. Many homes have fuel storage tanks. If the tanks are above ground, you can look at them to see what condition they are in. If you find no tank, ask if it is underground. If so, assume it is old, huge (2,000 gallons was common when fuel oil was inexpensive), and deteriorating. It could cave in, causing property damage or even injuries. Removal is expensive and is mandated by environmental regulations, so that you are not allowed to fill the tank with sand — not quite so expensive. Insurance seldom covers the cost of removal and soil clean-up. You will then need to buy an above-ground container and delivery pipes running to the furnace. Expect the cost and installation to be several hundred dollars. Most above ground tanks last about 30 years. It can be costly if a tank leaks; therefore, check for leaks or any other problems such as poor fuel flow to the furnace.

2

INSPECTING THE INSIDE OF THE HOME

Homes are inspected from the inside out. You want to work during the day and with bright flashlights so you have the best lighting. You want to take your time and look closely at everything. You do not want to miss something and have it come back to haunt you later. Don't forget to see the appendices and the companion CD-ROM for sample checklists and forms you can use to keep track of all your findings when inspecting a home.

FLOORS

While walking on the floors you need to check for uneven, sloped, bulging, or sagging floors. The entire floor sagging or sloping may be caused by the floor warping or shrinking over time. The house may have settled, or worst case, may still be settling so there is more damage to come. To look further into the potential problem, you should go underneath the floor and look-up. If the floor is sagging or sloping underneath too, you need to have a professional look for structural damage. Generally, floor supports are made of heartwood that will petrify without rotting. Good news!

Carpeting and any other kind of flooring can hide a multitude of sins. Be ready to remove a piece of the floor covering from a corner or two of each room to look at the floor itself. Check for water damage stains or rot, space between the floor and wall, and the material of the floor itself. Is it hardwood that has been maintained or merely plywood?

Is it moldy? Mold lives off anything that is or has been alive, such as wood. A portable handheld mold detector can confirm your suspicions. Concentrations of mold in indoor air samples should be similar to those found in the local outdoor air. Mold growth should be considered unacceptable because of potential health effects on building occupants and damage to buildings. Do not touch mold or moldy items with bare hands or get it into your eyes. Use personal protective equipment to prevent inhaling spores.

Chlorine is not effective on a continual basis as long as standing water collects on the area. To remove mold, remove the water at its source and discard whatever you can that is contaminated.

Is the carpeting padded? Is the padding worn? If the flooring is in bad shape, what is the cost of replacement? If you cannot see the floor at all, get a written statement from the owners about the material of the floor itself. If the owners assure you that the floor is hardwood, have them sign a statement that the floors are in good condition. You cannot know what the floors may look like and it can be quite costly to refinish hardwood floors, replace floors, and replace flooring.

If a tile floor has been laid directly on top of a concrete slab and the concrete slab was not packed correctly, it may settle down and cause a space between the floor and walls. This problem does need to be corrected. If not, the floor above may begin to sag because it does not have proper support.

WALLS

A look at interior walls of a house will give you indications of structural damage, the worst case scenario. Pay particular attention to the outside walls and those walls that support the roof or another floor that are "bearing" or support walls.

Check all the walls in the home for cracks, bulges, water stains, holes, and peeling paint. Those defects that are merely cosmetic can be dealt with by painting or using a wall covering, but cracks, warps, and water stains are evidence of more serious problems: the house settling, flooding, and/or holes in the roof that result in major, expensive repairs. You should determine the cause of the damage before proceeding any further.

Water seeping in from the outside causes visible water stains on walls that face the outside. Be sure to look for stains and peeling paint around the windows of a home indicating rotten, rusted, or unpainted window frames. Look to see if the window and door frames are level. If they are not, you need to get a professional to look at the problem. Some houses are simply not worth the cost of replacing windows and doors.

Walls inside the house may be made of wood or composition wood with various coverings, or they may have drywall nailed to the studs. Drywall is cheap, quick, easy to install, and imparts a certain fire protection. Old drywall betrays possible structural damage by staining, cracking, or bulging since it is made of gypsum, a soft, talc-like mineral.

If the home has wood paneling, take a couple of minutes to inspect it. Well built homes should have plasterboard beneath the wood paneling. To see if the walls are backed by plasterboard, find a space in the wall between the studs and press firmly against the wall. If the wall "gives" or pushes in, it is not backed by plasterboard — the thin wall paneling IS the wall.

This is the time for you to inquire about insulation in the wall, a good thing to have in all climates to save on heating and air conditioning bills.

The problem you need to be aware of with peeling paint is whether there is lead in it, which can harm children. Lead paint is found in older homes since its use was outlawed by federal legislation in 1978. This will be discussed more in Chapter 16.

Minor problems with walls are not hard to repair. This includes peeling paint (that is not lead based), small cracks, and holes. All they require is some spackle and paint.

CEILINGS

Inspect the ceilings in each room of the home as you did with walls, looking for cracks, peeling paint, and water stains that could indicate structural damage.

If a ceiling or its covering is bulging or sagging, you need to be concerned. If nothing else, this is a safety concern because if the ceiling is collecting water from leaky bathroom plumbing or a leaky roof, it could fall and land on someone, not to mention the expense of major repairs.

Do not automatically assume that a stain indicates a current problem — it may indicate a past problem that has already been fixed. If you spot discolorations, ask about them. Using a portable, inexpensive water meter, you can test the spot yourself to see if the moisture is still there. If the problem has been corrected, all you will need is paint to hide the stains. If it has not been fixed, you need to find the source of the water.

Water stains can come from a variety of sources. The most obvious one is the roof. A leaky roof can cause stains on the ceilings two or three floors below the top level. Other causes of ceiling stains are: leaky pipes, leaky seals or tile joints in the bathroom, or snow backing up under the shingles on the roof.

You also need to be aware that some homes have ceilings that are made from composition tiles. They are applied under plaster or a similar product and are connected together. They are usually made from fiberboard or glass fiber and may have been installed below a ceiling that was cracking or breaking apart. Be sure to look carefully at all sections of the tile ceiling to make sure they are not bulging or sagging. If they are, this may indicate that the ceiling behind the tiles is coming down, a major repair. The tiles need to be repaired as soon as possible. If they are not, more tiles around the loose ones can loosen other tiles until the ceiling falls down.

WINDOWS

Check every window for cracked or missing panes. Make sure all screens and storm windows are present and in good condition. Check the window frames to make sure they are in good shape and free of holes and cracks. Look at the window sill and the trim around the window to make sure there is no sign of rot or other damage. Also check to make sure the window fits in the frame correctly. You want to make sure there are no openings for water to get inside and that they are as air tight as possible.

As you inspect all the windows, you need to open each one to make sure it opens and shuts completely. Also, leave the windows open for a few seconds to make sure they stay open and do not start to slide back down. They may even crash back down so be careful.

There are many different types of windows that can be used in homes. Most homes will have more than one type. The main types of windows are double-hung, fixed, casement, jalousie, awning, horizontal and vertical sliders, and hopper.

Double-hung windows are one of the most popular types of windows on the market. They have separate sashes that slide up and down along on their own tracks. Check to make sure each window functions properly. Sometimes you will come across a single hung window that only has a lower window that slides.

Fixed windows have no operating mechanism. They usually have a wood frame around them and are easy to inspect. Just check the glass itself and the window frame to make sure there is no water damage.

Casement windows open and close with a crank. To inspect them, unlock them and turn the crank and see if they open and close completely. Check to see if the weather stripping is in place. If the handle slips while you are trying to open the window, do not force it. Give the window a little push. If it still does not open, just note that it will not open and move on.

Jalousie windows have several small panes that open and close together when a crank is turned. These windows all run parallel to the ground and allow a high amount of ventilation, but they do not seal tightly and usually are not weather-tight. In colder climates, jalousie windows should only be used on porches or in breezeways.

Awning windows have a hinge at the top and swing outward at the bottom. They are controlled by a lever or a crank and have a tendency to stick shut so make sure they open properly. Check the area surrounding the window for air spaces.

Horizontal and vertical sliders are cheaper windows that usually have aluminum frames. Make sure to check if the vertical sliders work because they become clogged with dirt and other junk and prevent the window from opening. Also, because aluminum has a tendency to sweat, condensation can drip down and damage the wood around the frame. Be sure to pay special attention to the condition of the wood around the frame.

Hopper windows swing inward from the top. These are popular in basements. Be sure the glass is in good shape. Try opening and closing each of these windows. Also, the handle that opens each window should be tight and stay in place so that the window does not open unexpectedly.

You will also need to examine the windows from the outside of the home for any obvious defects. Windows are expensive to replace as we will discuss in Chapter 11.

DOORS

Be sure to look at the doors from the outside as well as the inside. Doors are often overlooked by potential home buyers and they usually cost several hundred dollars. Pay special attention to the appearance of the front door as it creates a first impression.

Check that the doors are solid and sturdy. Make sure they open and close correctly. Check to see if the door seals completely.

If part of the door seals well but another part does not seal then either the door is warped or the door frame is out of plumb. Also, check the locks and make sure they work correctly. You will probably want to replace the locks before you move in anyway, but you should still check to see if all the locks work properly. Do not forget to check the glass in the door, the hinges, and the entire surface of the door for scratches, holes, or other imperfections.

Doors made of solid wood look great but they tend to deteriorate easily. Solid-wood doors warp, split, rot, and crack. Also, most wood doors do not insulate against cold weather well so check the condition of the storm door and insulation strips as well.

A steel door provides greatest protection from outside elements, although the bottom of the door may corrode. In colder climates when salt is thrown on the doorstep to melt ice, it gets in the door and damages it. Also make sure there is no trim missing or falling apart that would allow foam insulation inside the door to fall out. Finally, check the weather stripping that goes around the door. It is magnetic and can get ripped out over time.

Fiberglass doors need to be checked for obvious fading and for fiberglass splinters. You should look closely for any tiny splinters that stick out of the door. Do not touch or you may get an annoying splinter in your finger.

Storm doors are placed on the outside of the door. Check them the same as the other doors but pay special attention to the damper arm that runs from the door to the door frame to close the door if it is left open. Make sure it is in good shape, functions properly, and is not bent or damaged in any other way.

Interior doors in the home will be lighter and are not as important or as expensive as exterior doors. When checking these doors, make sure they latch, open, and lock correctly. Do not forget to check behind the door to see if the knob has damaged the wall.

OUTLETS AND LIGHTING FIXTURES

Check each room to be sure the electrical outlets have no wires sticking out and that the receptacles are not broken in any other way. You can test outlets using a basic plug-in tester. Be aware of how many outlets are in each room and where they are located. In older homes there are sometimes few outlets. While this is not a huge problem it can be annoying and could be dangerous if you are forced to use extension cords to power most things in the house.

Check the kitchen and bathroom to make sure the outlets near any water source (tub, sinks) are ground fault circuit interrupters (GFCI). It is easy to identify GFCI outlets because they include an obvious reset or test button. It is important to have this type of outlet around water because it will shut off the electricity if an appliance comes into contact with water. It can save your life if you accidentally drop the hair dryer into a sink with water in it.

You should also check all the lighting fixtures throughout the house. If you want to and you have the time, you can go through the house turning every light on. You can even bring a low watt bulb to check fixtures that do not light. Check the overall condition of the fixtures making sure there are no obvious problems like loose wires.

Just as you did with the outlets, check each room to see how many light fixtures there are. Make sure there are lights over sinks and near fixed mirrors. There should also be lights over stairs and anywhere else you think they are needed.

If you have any problem with your outlets, make sure you get a professional to check them out and fix them, if necessary. Any work that involves electricity should always be done by someone who knows exactly what he or she is doing.

HEAT REGISTERS

The location of the heat registers and radiators is important. They should be located near windows or a door on the exterior wall of the room so that warm air counteracts any cold air slipping into the home via the windows or the door. Their placement will reduce drafts and also minimize cold spots in the room.

You may also find space heaters in the home. These are stand alone heaters that are designed to heat three rooms at the most. Other than fireplaces or wood stoves, most area heaters are either electric or gas-fired. Gas heaters distribute heat better than electric heaters.

There are three types of electrical space heaters: baseboard, wall, and radiant or panel heating.

Electric baseboard heaters use resistance coils for heating. They are easy, fairly inexpensive to install, and are good at heating the room evenly.

Wall heaters are small and usually have a fan to push warm air into a room. They are usually used in garages or in a workshop. They do not heat evenly and are commonly turned by hand.

Radiant or panel heating is similar to baseboard heating. The big difference is that panel heating uses circulating water to heat the room instead of coils.

You should make sure there is some heat source in every room. Also look for the location of the thermostat or thermostats. Obviously, the more thermostats in the home the easier it will be to control the temperature and the more money you can save on your heating and cooling bills. Being able to keep different sections of your home at different temperatures is called zone heating and is handy and cost effective in climates with extreme temperatures.

Finally, check each register or radiator for damage. Be sure they are in working condition and that there are no signs of leakage on the floor around or beneath the registers or radiators. If you have any questions or concerns about any part of the heating, consult a professional. Heating will be discussed further in Chapter 9.

House Inspection Tip #3

Always check the walls of every room to see if there are any cracks or bulges. Also look to see whether the paint or wallpaper may be peeling. If you find these problems, know that it will cost more money to repair them.

3

THE KITCHEN

The kitchen is where your family will tend to congregate. It is important to have a kitchen that fits your needs or else you will suffer daily irritations and aggravations. Don't forget to see the appendices and the companion CD-ROM for sample checklists and forms you can use to keep track of all your findings when inspecting a home.

THE KITCHEN SINK

You should check the water flow from the faucet and the drainage of the sink. Make sure both work correctly. Look for cracks and any other blemishes on the sink itself. Make sure it is in working condition and is securely fastened. Finally, if it has a sprayer connected to it, make sure it works.

While the water is running, turn the spout from side to side to see that it swivels smoothly. Then gently lift the spout and make sure there is no leak from under the spout or the faucet. Check the condition of all faucet handles and make sure they do not grind as you turn them.

When checking the faucet, you should see a strong flow of water from each (hot and cold) tap. A faucet with good water pressure will produce about four gallons of water per minute. There could be any number of reasons for a lack of pressure: deposits in water pipes, a bend in the pipe, or pipes that are too small in diameter. It could be caused by the faucet aerator's being clogged and needing cleaning. You can unscrew the aerator from the end of the faucet spout and check its condition while you are there.

Remember to check the faucet for both hot and cold water. Check each of them separately. Quickly turn the faucet off and on a few times. If you hear a knock when the water is abruptly turned off, it means the water is causing a vibration that could damage the pipes or the fittings.

Check for leaks while the water is flowing through the faucet. Be sure to check behind the faucet and all around the sink. After you turn off the water, look to see if water drips from behind the faucet. Also, take note of whether the faucet continues to drip after being turned off. Make sure the faucet is higher than the overflow rim on the sink. If the faucet is lower, dirty water can back up into your clean water line.

Look under the sink to see what kind of trap it has. There are two types of traps: a "P" trap and an "S" trap. A "P" trap looks like a hook or a cane on its side while an "S" trap dips down and then goes up before going back down — like an "S" on its side. You want to see if your trap is properly ventilated. One test you can perform is to fill the sink with water and then let the water out. As the sink empties, if you hear a sucking sound then the trap is not ventilated properly.

Also, check below the sink for automatic shut off valves. They are not mandatory, but they will come in handy at some point.

If there is a garbage disposal in the kitchen, run the water and turn the disposal switch on. If nothing happens, it is broken. If it makes a high-pitched squealing noise, its bearings are bad. If it only hums instead of grinding, it is probably locked. If there is a hammering sound, there could be something caught in the disposal. Do not try to fix the problem or unclog it. Just note its condition and move on.

You also need to ask whether the garbage disposal was installed after the house was built. This is a concern if your house uses a septic tank for waste. Find out if the tank was made to have a garbage disposal pumping waste into it.

COUNTERTOPS

There are many different types of countertops intended for kitchens. Some of the more popular ones are laminate, stone, wood, and ceramic. Inspection is the same for all types.

Check for major defects, such as cracks, scratches, and other marks on the countertop. Stains on the surface may indicate that hot pans were set on a countertop that could not withstand heat.

Check for gaps between the sink and counter. Make sure water has not seeped in between the sink and counter rotting the wood anywhere around the sink. Press down firmly on the counter for soft spots where the water may have seeped in.

Make sure you have the amount of counter space that you need. If you spend time cooking regularly, you will need a sufficient amount of counter space. Be sure the home meets your needs.

CABINETS

Check the outside of the cabinets for damaged or missing doors and hardware. Look inside the cabinets and check the shelves. Make sure the shelves are sturdy and able to bear the weight of pots and canned goods. Pay particular attention to the cabinets that are directly below and beside the kitchen sink for water damage. Does the number of cabinets in the kitchen meet your needs?

ELECTRICAL SYSTEM

The kitchen should have the more electrical outlets than any other room in the house and they should be located in the places convenient to your small appliances. The kitchen should also have more electrical circuits — one for the major appliances and one for everything else. Older homes may not be wired adequately. To tell if it is, you can go to the electric panel (breaker) box and check the labeling for the circuits. If you do not trust the labels, you can find out for yourself by throwing circuit breakers and checking to see where the power is lost. To save time, plug a radio into a kitchen outlet and turn it up loud. Then throw breakers until the music stops. Leave that breaker off and then go back to the kitchen. Plug the radio into the other outlets in the room. If any of them have power then there are two circuits.

The first type of outlet you might find in the kitchen is the two-prong receptacle. This type of plug is not grounded. It is not a violation because they have been grandfathered in so they are legal but not necessarily safe.

The duplex three-prong grounded receptacle is another type of outlet you might find in the kitchen. Do not take it for granted that these outlets are grounded. Sometimes they are just three-prong grounded receptacles that have been hooked into wires for a two prong receptacle — a violation. Use a plug-in tester to check whether an outlet is grounded. If it is not, the light indicating an ungrounded receptacle will light up. This test will not work if the outlet has a false grounding wire, a wire running from the terminal of the outlet to the neutral terminal. You can see this wire if you open the outlet or you can use a digital circuit tester to see if the receptacle is not grounded correctly.

Another type of outlet is a duplex three prong with a ground fault breaker. Again, check that the outlet really has a ground fault breaker and that it works correctly. Simply press in the button and listen for a loud click. That sound is the breaker popping out. If it does not click, it probably does not work correctly.

The fourth type of receptacle is a ground fault circuit interrupter (GFCI). As mentioned in Chapter 2, it is essential around sinks and other sources of water. Make sure the GFCI is working correctly. Insert the plug-in tester and push the test button. The outlet should trip. Be sure to test each outlet in the kitchen. They should all have GFCI or be built around the outlet that has GFCI. To check this, trip the one receptacle with GFCI and check to see if the other outlets are working. If they still work, you will need to update the receptacles so that all the countertop outlets have GFCI.

You should also examine the other outlets in the kitchen. Major appliances are required by law to be grounded without exception. Check to make sure all the appliances — especially the refrigerator — are plugged into grounded outlets. Again, do not assume an outlet is grounded just because it is a duplex three prong. Check it with a plug-in tester or a digital circuit tester.

You do not want your refrigerator plugged into an outlet that is GFCI. You do not want the GFCI tripping and stopping your refrigerator from working. GFCI outlets can be touchy and can trip at any time. You do not want your food to spoil because of a GFCI tripped without your knowledge and for no reason.

Remember to check the lighting in the kitchen. Be sure the switches work and that there is sufficient lighting around the places you will be working, eating, and preparing foods. Make sure the switches are in logical places as well. Do not assume the switches are easily accessible; find them and make sure they work correctly.

APPLIANCES

You want to check any appliances that are going to stay in the house when you purchase it. We already discussed how to check the garbage disposal. Other appliances you may need to check include the stove, refrigerator, and dishwasher. Though a clothes washer and dryer may be in the kitchen, these appliances will be addressed in Chapter 10.

To check the stove, turn it on and make sure each burner or element works. If it is a gas stove and you can get to the gas line, check for gas leaks around the fittings. You can do this using a gas sniffer.

Turn on both the light and the exhaust fan above the stove to make sure they are operational.

If the refrigerator is on, check inside to make sure it is cool and check the freezer to make sure its temperature is below freezing. It may have been turned off by the owner. Push on the floor around the refrigerator and make sure there are no soft spots. Also, check to make sure the seal (gasket) on the door is not worn or rotted. To test it, stick a dollar bill in the door and close the door. You should encounter resistance when you pull the bill out. Continue to do this all around the door.

Check the dishwasher for leaks. Visually check the floor to make sure there is no warping or discoloration. Then run the dishwasher. Make sure it fills with water, turns off, and drains the water. While it is running, check to make sure there is no water dripping through the seal on the door.

House Inspection Tip #4

Turn on any faucets, watch the color of the water, how long it takes for hot water to get there, and whether the sink drains easily. Check under the sink for any moisture from leaky drains. Also make sure to inspect all appliances included in the sale.

4

THE BATHROOM

Water damage is the greatest threat to a bathroom. In this chapter we will review over the different aspects of the bathroom to review when inspecting a home you are considering purchasing. Don't forget to see the appendices and the companion CD-ROM for sample checklists and forms you can use to keep track of all your findings when inspecting a home.

TUB/SHOWER

Most of the moisture damage that happens in bathrooms is caused by improper ventilation. The tub and shower cause moisture to build up in the room. If there is not an exhaust fan to pull the moisture out, it will damage the floors and walls.

Most of the time an exhaust fan is not required by codes if there is a window that opens to the outside in the bathroom. However, a properly installed exhaust fan should be in every bathroom, and it should always be used when the shower is going.

A properly installed exhaust fan should discharge the exhaust into the outside air. It may be difficult but try to locate where the exhaust is going. The exhaust should discharge through ducts on either at the side of the house or on the roof. Sometimes it discharges into the attic. This is a problem because it can cause moisture problems there.

To check for moisture damage, look for lines on the wall that have been caused by water droplets running down and staining the paint. You should also look for wet drywall or peeling wall paper. If the moisture problem is really bad you might see rotting walls or a rotting ceiling.

Another cause of moisture in the bathroom could be water coming in around the tub or shower faucet. Check the faucet and the handle closely. If it was not sealed correctly, water will leak behind and damage the drywall causing major problems. To check it, look closely for little gaps or cracks where water could seep in. Also if the tub or shower is tiled, check carefully to make sure the grout is not missing or cracked between the tiles.

Another effect of too much moisture is rusty metal fixtures. Check baseboard heaters and light fixtures and look for corrosion or signs of pitting. If a cheap light fixture has even a little bit of rust, it can easily be ruined.

You should look for any sign of leaking from the tub or shower. Find the panel that gives access to the supply pipes for the tub or shower. This panel is usually located on the wall behind the tub or shower faucets. If there is not one, whenever work needs to be done the repair person will have to rip into the wall. If there is one, open the panel and watch the pipes for leaking while you run the faucet and then the shower. At this point, check for water pressure.

Check the faucet and showerhead to make sure they are secure to the wall. If the showerhead is loose, it could cause problems, including snapping a pipe.

If there is a spa or whirlpool in the bathroom, fill the unit with enough water to cover the jets or the ports. As new water runs into the unit, it is mixing with old water that has been sitting stagnant for quite sometime. Do not allow your hands or arms to touch the water because it is dirty with bacteria. If you do touch the water, be sure to wash with antibacterial soap. If you see black particles floating in the water, you need to get the lines cleaned before using the unit.

You may want to have a professional to check out the spa or whirlpool if you are at all concerned. All units should be equipped with some sort of GFCI. A professional will be able to tell you the condition of the unit and what it would cost for you to fix it, if needed.

THE TOILET

Check for any damage to the tank or toilet bowl. Even the smallest crack could leak at any time. Next check the shutoff valve for any sign of water leakage. There may be condensation that has built up on the valve so wipe it off and check it. Then check the supply tube the same way you checked the shut off valve.

Take off the top of the toilet tank. If the water level is all the way up to the overflow tube, it may mean that the refill mechanism is running too long, causing the toilet to run continually. While you still have the top of the tank off, listen for dripping water. If you hear water dripping, it probably means water is escaping below the rubber seal in the tank and out into the toilet bowl.

Flush the toilet while you still have the top off the tank. It should flush smoothly without undue noise. The tank should empty and refill fairly quickly. If you see a slimy, red coating in the tank, (or anywhere else in the house) it is red algae, which is actually a bacteria that is hard to remove.

After you check the tank and replace the lid, test the toilet to make sure it is tight against the floor. If it is not, it may be leaking sewer gases. Sniff the air to see if you smell anything if you suspect the toilet is not affixed to the floor. If the toilet rocks back and forth, it could mean a few different things. If water did not leak out onto the floor when the toilet was flushed, it probably does not have a broken seal. It could rock because the screws that fasten the toilet to the floor are not tight enough, or it could mean that the flange is broken or the floor itself is rotten. Press down firmly on the floor to check if it is soft, indicating rot.

Check the back of the toilet for signs of water caused by condensation or by a leak from the toilet tank. The tank could be leaking at the hold-down bolts or where the tank runs into the bowl. Whether it is condensation or a leak, if there is water you have to make sure the floor is not rotting or already rotten.

The toilet seat should not be a major concern as they are inexpensive and easy to install.

THE SINK

You need to check the bathroom sink and the vanity the same way you checked the kitchen sink and counters. Check the faucet, the sink, the drains, and the water lines. Look for signs of leaking and rotting. Check the water pressure and make sure the sink fills and drains properly. Also make sure that there is a "P" trap under the sink. "S" traps are no longer allowed in bathrooms because they siphon often and then allow sewer gas into the home. They have been grandfathered in though so if you are inspecting an older home you might find an "S" trap. Know that if you buy a home with an "S" trap in the bathroom, there is a good chance you will smell sewer gas occasionally.

It the bathroom has a sink directly attached to the wall, a wall-hung sink, make sure it is fastened tightly and not tilting toward the floor. A sink that is loose and tilting can cause the drain and water supply lines to move and leak.

A pedestal sink is attached to the wall by the bowl and has a stand giving it support from below. Make sure everything is secure and that the sink does not move around. Check the back of the sink for leaks and for the "P" trap. You will probably need a flashlight and a mirror to help you see behind the sink.

As you did with the other faucets, make sure the handles work well. Look for water leaking from the handles or from behind the faucet. Finally, make sure that both the hot and cold water works. Remember to try each temperature separately.

ELECTRICAL

There may not be many electrical outlets in the bathroom. Make sure there are at least two so that certain grooming can be performed. Any outlet in the bathroom should be a ground fault circuit interrupter (GFCI) to protect you from electrocution. Remember to make sure that the receptacle is truly a GFCI. Do not take it for granted just because it appears to be in working condition. Test it with a plug-in tester. GFCI outlets and the electricity in the home were discussed in the previous chapters and will be discussed again in Chapter 6.

5

THE BASEMENT / CRAWL SPACE

You want to spend the most time inspecting the basement and the things housed within it such as the furnace and hot water heater. The condition of the basement affects the rest of the house either sooner or later. Don't forget to see the appendices and the companion CD-ROM for sample checklists and forms you can use to keep track of all your findings when inspecting a home.

FINISHED OR UNFINISHED BASEMENT

A basement may be finished, unfinished, or partially finished. A finished basement has regular walls and a ceiling where people are able to live just as they do in the main part of the house. In an unfinished basement, the walls and floor are concrete and the studs are visible. You will also see the plumbing, duct work, and wiring overhead. Partially finished basements have some walls and a carpet on the floor but still show signs of being a bare basement. If the floor is still bare concrete, the basement is generally considered unfinished. The exception to this is if the floor has been covered with epoxy coating. A finished basement requires that all outlets be GFCI.

If the basement is partially finished, you will want to look at the work that has been completed. At some point you may want to finish the work that someone else started. You will want to know if the work that was done is worth keeping or if it will need to be replaced. A partially finished basement that has been poorly constructed will cost you more time and money than a completely unfinished basement would. Therefore, do not assume that a partially finished basement is better than an unfinished basement.

Check the drywall first. Make sure they are all taped and not damaged. Make sure the walls are sturdy and not bulging or showing other signs of damage. Look at the receptacle boxes to see if they are too far out from the wall or too far into the wall. Analyze everything and it should be easy to determine if the job was done well done.

STRUCTURAL

It is much easier to inspect the structure of a house by checking an unfinished basement because you can see the condition of the bare joists. Check for sagging and look for any joists that have been cut away to string wiring or pipes. No more than one third of the edge of the joist should ever be removed.

Walk around the entire basement and look at all the joists. Check the joists for water damage or any other kind of visible damage. You also need to look for insects in and around the joists.

Do not forget to examine the stairs that lead back up to the main part of the home. Make sure they are sturdy and not rotting or deteriorating. Check the hand rail and the lowest step to make sure it is not a shorter or taller step than all the rest. You do not want anyone to trip going up or down the steps.

Note whether there are bare nail tips in the ceiling of the basement and make sure to bend them with a hammer so that any child jumping up and down will not be injured.

WALLS

Check around the basement for any signs of flooding such as damp or muddy walls or puddles on the floor. If there is standing water in a basement, do not walk into it as it might be electrified. Even if the floor is dry, you may be able to see signs of past flooding. Look at the walls and appliances in the basement and check to see if there are any horizontal lines or rings left by flooding.

Another way to tell if a basement has water problems is to look for a white residue on the walls. This white powdery substance is the minerals left behind from water that seeped back out of the basement. It will especially show up in the corners of the basement, but it may also be visible on leather furniture and anything made out of plastic.

You may not think it is important that a basement has a water problem. It becomes a big problem when mildew and mold grow because of the damp conditions. Mildew has a distinct musty smell that you can detect long before wood begins to rot. Mold spores are too small to see while they are floating in the air. When they settle on something organic and moist to feed on, they become visible. They can settle in your lungs and cause problems including severe allergies, illness, and even death.

It is much more difficult to tell if a finished basement has water problems. The leakage may be occurring behind the finished walls. Look at the bottom of all the walls for stains or any other sign of water damage. These signs include crumbling of the wall, stains, or rotting paneling, and mildew on the walls. Another clue to whether the basement is dry is to simply take notice of how it feels. Does it feel damp to you?

Also, check to see if there is a dehumidifier in the basement and if it is working.

When looking for sources of water that seeps into the basement, check the window wells for standing water. Look for stains on the walls below the windows.

A major source of water could be a stairwell. If it is outside, it should have a drain at the bottom. Water will run down into the stairwell and if it does not have anywhere else to go, it will go into the basement. The drain should be free of leaves or anything that can stop water from running through it. The drain may also be plugged somewhere you cannot see. Check the walls around the landing of the stairwell for lines indicating flooding. If you want to be sure that the drain works, take a hose and run some water down it.

Your next area of concern for water leakage should be the walls running parallel to the rain gutters. If gutters are not clean or are broken, water saturates the ground around the foundation. Since basement walls are porous, water will seep right in. Downspouts that are not depositing rainwater far enough away from the house can cause basement problems. They can also become blocked and backup, causing rainwater to collect next to the house and eventually seep into the basement.

Even if you find no evidence of water seepage and the rain gutters look fine, you need to remember to check them occasionally if you move into the home. Some gutters are built too long without enough downspouts. This could cause the gutters to overflow or buckle under the weight of all the rainwater. The result is water falling next to the house. Also, make sure your gutters do not become clogged causing water to build up at one end of the gutter resulting in rainwater leaking down beside your house. The problem of clogging can be taken care of by simply cleaning your gutters once or twice a year.

In colder climates, freeze cracks occur along horizontal lines from water seeping into the basement wall, freezing, and expanding, thus splitting the wall, subsequently letting rainwater into the basement.

Sometimes a section of the basement wall can no longer take the weight that is bearing on it, causing part of the wall to crack and eventually begin to bow under the pressure. Then water flows into the basement either in torrents or in little places of seepage. Look for places that might have been patched over in an attempt to stop the seeping. Eventually the patch will fail and the opening will grow larger, leading to great deal of damage to the wall. To stop the water you will have to divert it from the other side of the wall.

Another popular place for water to get in is where the basement wall meets the basement floor. Water travels down the outside wall of the basement and over time seeps into the basement and pools on the floor.

BASEMENT FLOOR

Walk around the entire basement and look for major cracks. Minor cracks are in almost all basements and should not be a concern for you. Larger cracks are not necessarily a problem at the moment but could become a problem at some point. Also, look for signs of pipe leaks and pipe breaks. There will be either colorful stains or a stain on the floor.

Floors that are finished usually have indoor/outdoor carpeting, cloth carpeting, or linoleum. Pay special attention to the edge of the floor covering near the walls where stains will be most apparent. The carpet may even be squishy if the carpet pad has soaked up water. Tile and linoleum squares may be loose from standing water.

Check for a sump pump. Older pumps are down in a hole with a rod and motor above the hole. The pump turns on and pumps out the water from the sump pit when the rod is lifted by water in the hole. To test whether the sump pump works, all you have to do is lift the rod.

Submersible pumps are newer. The entire pump is inside the hole, and they work by rising water moving a sensor on the pump, causing it to turn on.

All sump pumps have a large pipe that runs from the pump to the outside or to the house's sewer line. You need to make sure the water is goes far enough from the house so that it does not just run right back into the basement. Also, in most municipalities it is against codes to have pump water running into public sewerage because it can overload the system.

To test the sump pump, run a hose into the hole. It should turn on and pump the water out. Listen to make sure it does not make any high pitched noises and that there is no water spraying out of the pump. If the sump pump is a diaphragm pump without a rod, it will have a container as a part of the pump that turns on when it fills with water. Again, just run water into this type of pump until it reaches the point where the drain pours into the hole. More water may result in the pump's overflowing.

FLOOR DRAINS

Basement floor drains should be in most basements, unless the house is built on a hill and sufficiently drains water away from the home. Even so, basement drains can prove to be handy. For example, if a pipe bursts and fills your basement with water, it will be difficult to get the water out if you do not have a floor drain or a sump pump.

Be aware that floor drains often do not work. To check one, simply use a hose to run water down the drain. It could take a few minutes for the drain to back-up so that you can see that it is not actually draining. If you can, question the owner about how well the drain works. It is possible for water to run down one drain and then come back out of a different drain.

You will need to ask where the floor drains empty. Some are allowed to empty into a sewer and can cause a problem with sewer gasses coming up out of the drain if there is trouble with trap evaporation. You can reverse it by pouring mineral oil onto the seal. Other drains stop this problem by remaining primed all the time from the discharged water of a clothes washer or dishwasher.

Check for a heat pump in the basement. If there is, you need to check where the condensation drain goes when it leaves the pump. The lines could go anywhere including under the slab of the basement or to the outside wall of the basement. If they go only as far as the other side of the basement wall, they could cause the drainage to travel down the wall and back into the basement.

BASEMENT LIGHTING

There needs to be sufficient lighting in the basement especially around stairs. Make sure there is a switch at the top and at the bottom of the stairs. If the basement is unfinished and one switch controls all the lights in the basement, make sure the switch is located somewhere at the top of the stairs leading into the basement. You do not want to stumble down the stairs every time you enter the basement. The means used to turn on the lights can be anything (switch, pull string) as long as the basement is not finished. If there is no lighting in the basement, take note of this. It is especially a problem if there are things in the basement that may need servicing, such as a furnace or hot water heater.

If the basement is finished, there should be switched lighting at every place of entrance. Make sure all light fixtures have a bulb in them. You do not want anyone putting their finger into an open socket that is hot. You will also be able to tell whether all the light fixtures work. If you have a low watt bulb with you, try it in all the sockets. If there are fluorescent fixtures in the basement, they may take a while to turn on. Fluorescent lights do not work well in a moist environment because the terminals corrode easily. If the fluorescent lights take a long time to light or just flash on and off continuously, take note that they are not functioning correctly.

POINTS OF ENTRY

We have already discussed interior-exterior entry ways into the basement. You need to make sure that exterior entry ways have a drain in the landing at the bottom of the stairs or outside any entry way. You also need to make sure it is working properly. You should analyze the door. Make sure it shuts and locks. Also, make sure it does not have any spaces and that it is sealed well.

Make sure the stairs are sturdy with no signs of rot. They should be spaced properly with a reliable rail.

CRAWL SPACE

Crawl spaces should be inspected the same as basements. If the crawl space is too low or if there is no entry point, take note of it. Do not put yourself into a bad situation. You should try to shine your flashlight into the crawl space to see if there are any obvious problems.

If you are able to enter the crawl space, you should wear a pair of coveralls and bring along a strong flashlight. You want to be able to see as much as possible but because crawl spaces do not have concrete flooring, they may be muddy or dusty. Newer homes usually have a plastic covering on the ground that will help protect the insulation and the wood from moisture. If the house does not have a tarp in the crawl space, you should put one under there if you decide to live in the house. Insulation in homes without a tarp often falls down onto the ground because of all the moisture it absorbs.

There should also be vent openings for the crawl space to help cut down on moisture. If there is a ground covering in the crawl space, there should be a vent opening of one square foot for every

1,500 square feet of living area. If there is no ground covering, there should be at least one vent opening on each side of the house. If there is not or if the vent openings have been covered over permanently, you can expect to have moisture problems that will sooner or later lead to bigger problems with the structure of the home.

Within the crawl space inspect the walls, posts, piers, and wood-support framing for rotting and other evidence of damage from water or any other source. Also check the insulation between the floor joists. Almost all crawl spaces are not heated so that insulation is needed. If not, heat will be lost through the floor. If there is insulation, make sure the side facing the floor has a vapor barrier. Additional moisture can enter the crawl space from the house if the barrier is not there. If there is enough condensation from the house that travels down through the floor and into the insulation, the insulation is worthless. If you find some sections that have missing or loose insulation, make a note of it and make sure you fix the problem.

While you are checking the insulation, look at the joists for any sign of decay or insect infestation. Most of the time it is the low crawl spaces that have problems with rotting and sagging because of the amount of moisture that collects in the crawl spaces. However, if the crawl space is not sufficiently ventilated, the stagnant moist air will produce a great deal of condensation that will moisten the floor joists and cause them to begin rotting away.

You should also check pipes and drains that run underneath the floors of the house for leaks. Do not mistake condensation for a leaky pipe or drain. All pipes should be intact, supported every few feet, with no sagging between supports. There should not be different types of plastic used on the same pipe either. If pipes and heating ducts are not insulated, you may need to insulate them if you choose to live in the house. You do not want to risk having pipes freeze in the winter. (Chapter 7 contains more tips about how to inspect water pipes and drains.)

Some houses have both a basement and a section of the house that is only crawl space. If the crawl space is hooked into a basement, it does not need to have vents on the side. You need to make sure that the crawl space is not walled off from the basement, though. Even if the basement looks great with no signs of seepage or any other damage, you still need to inspect the crawl space, which could have problems that the basement does not, or it could reveal problems that have been covered up.

Be aware that some problems can be covered up during the short period of time a house is on the market. For example, it is easy to paint over water stains. That is why it is important to ask the owner questions about the history of the basement. Also, check over the disclosure statement. Look for places that may have been forgotten about, like the back side of doors or behind furnaces or water heaters.

You will probably need to inspect other things in the basement while you are down there. This includes electrical wiring, plumbing, septic, furnaces, hot water heaters, clothes washers, and other appliances. (All of these things will be discussed in detail in one of the following chapters.)

House Inspection Tip #5

Look in the basement or crawl space to see if there is any standing
water or any stains that indicate that there was once standing
water. Look at the floor to see if it is in good condition. Is there any
indication of rotting or sagging floor beams?

6

ELECTRICAL WIRING

A home should have electrical wiring running to every room. If it is not run correctly, it may be a mere inconvenience (always tripping a circuit breaker because too many outlets run into the same circuit) or a tragedy (a fire that destroys your home). Therefore, it is important that you understand how electrical wiring works and how to inspect it properly. Don't forget to see the appendices and the companion CD-ROM for sample checklists and forms you can use to keep track of all your findings when inspecting a home.

ELECTRICAL SERVICE/CAPACITY

Make sure no tree branches touch wires running into the home. They could wear away the protective cover, leaving wires bare and dangerous. Tree branches that are too close to the wires or touching the wires should be trimmed away.

You also need to make sure the wires are connected to the house and that the outer protection is in good shape. Often the wires running down the house into the meter box are the homeowner's responsibility. If they are frayed or worn out in any way they need to be fixed. Check to see if it is the homeowner's responsibility or the utility company's job and then plan accordingly. Just be sure they are replaced before they create a hazardous situation.

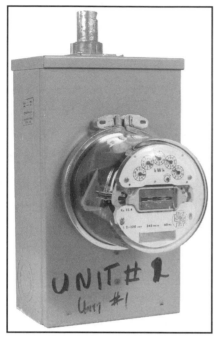

No matter what type of electrical wires they are, underground or above ground, they will stop at the meter box. The meter may be located outside or inside the home. From the meter box, the wires run into the panel box, also known as the service switch, which is where all the electricity branches out to all the parts of the house.

Electrical capacity for a house is important because it can be annoying if you always have to shut off the dishwasher to run the vacuum cleaner, for example. Therefore, you need to make sure the electrical capacity in the home is sufficient.

If you have special needs or if you are still wondering if the house has enough electrical capacity, you can find a chart that lists all the equipment you will want to run and how much power they each require. Then you can figure out exactly what you will need and whether you will have to upgrade the service.

PANEL BOX

The panel (breaker or fuse) box can be located inside or outside the house. The most common place is inside the home, usually in the basement. If the panel box is outside, check to see if it is susceptible to rain. Usually anything that is not covered by a roof needs to be in a weather tight panel box that is rated for outdoor use with a solid front usually hinged at the top. The front panel is lifted and will normally reveal another door that is hinged on the side.

The panel box should be easily accessible. It should not be covered up or have anything in front of it, including workbenches. All people, short or tall, thin or overweight, should be able to get to the panel box easily.

Inside the panel box there will be either fuses or circuit breakers. Fuses need to screw into the panel box. When a fuse blows, you will need to unscrew it and replace it with a new one. Circuit breakers are much easier to deal with. When they overload, instead of blowing, they just trip like a light switch. The switch goes from the "on" position to "off," stopping electricity to the circuit. All you need to do is switch the breaker back to the "on" position.

Home fires usually start with an overloaded circuit. That is why fuses and circuit breakers are so important. As soon as the circuit is overloaded, the fuse will blow or the circuit will trip. Sometimes the circuit breaker switch sticks in the "on" position, not tripping when it should, causing a disaster. Therefore, manually trip the breakers to make sure they work and continue to check them regularly.

If the panel box has fuses, you need to make sure you replace a blown fuse with a fuse that has the same capacity. If you replace it with a lower capacity, the fuse will blow when it does not actually need to do so. A bigger problem arises when you replace a blown fuse with a fuse of a larger capacity, making it so the fuse does not blow when it should. In this case, the wires become hot from carrying too much electricity, starting a fire. Be sure you are careful to replace fuses with identical fuses. You can help protect yourself from making a mistake by inserting a fustat into all the openings to allow only the correct size fuse to be inserted into each place. The fustat will only allow you to screw in the type of fuse that belongs in each individual spot.

The panel box itself should have a cover on it and may have some sort of door that will either swing out or up. Never remove the cover from a panel box. It is not much different than leaving a gun around for others to find. Children can get into a panel box without a cover and seriously hurt themselves.

Study the cover on the panel box and make sure there are no missing filler plates or fuses. Filler plates are the plates that get knocked out so that breakers can be put into the panel. Any fuses or filler plates that are missing provide an opportunity for someone, especially a child, to stick a finger into the vacant spot and be electrocuted. Be sure to keep everything covered at all times.

As a general rule, every panel box should have at least one 15-amp lighting circuit and two 20-amp appliance circuits for every 500 square feet of living area. If the panel box has fuses, look around for blown fuses. If there are some, one of the circuits is constantly being overloaded and blowing its fuse. This could mean that more branch circuits need to be installed.

There are certain parts of the panel box that can be dangerous and should be checked only by an electrician or a certified home inspector. Avoid any in-depth inspection inside the panel box. Leave it up to the professionals.

Be careful when you open the panel box. You should be wearing safety goggles to protect yourself from sparks or sudden fire. The panel box should be attached with special screws that have blunt ends. Not just any type of screw can be used; the screws must be specific to the panel box. You should also make sure that the cables running into the panel box are protected by NM connectors (strain relievers).

Look at what type of wiring is used. It should be copper wiring but it may be aluminum which was occasionally used for wiring between 1965 and 1973. While it was acceptable to use aluminum wiring then, it was later discovered that became too hot and actually started fires. In fact, aluminum wiring that was installed before 1972 is 55 times more likely to reach a hazardous level of heating than copper wiring. There are two easy ways to identify aluminum wiring. If you can see the actual wiring, it will appear silver in color. You can also look closely at the plastic wire jacket to see if there word "aluminum" is stamped on it.

All the aluminum wiring should be replaced with copper wiring. If you spot aluminum wiring, you need to hire an electrician to inspect your home and update the wiring where it is needed. If you suspect the house may have aluminum wiring, consult an electrician.

Make sure the panel box is not overloaded. There should be no more than one wire under each breaker screw. Also, look for one wire going from the main panel box and feeding another panel box. This is known as an illegal feeder and will need to be remedied as soon as possible. Do not confuse a secondary panel box with a box that is used to protect the wiring from a surge from lightning.

If you run across a panel box that is overloaded, be careful. It will probably be a mass of wires all clumped together. Be especially careful when you remove and replace the panel cover. When replacing the panel cover, make sure you do not trap any wires between the cover and the panel box.

GROUNDING

The electrical system in the house must the grounded, which means that some of the wiring in the panel box is connected to a rod that runs directly into the ground. You should check to make sure that there is a ground rod, but be aware that instead of a ground rod the grounding may be taken care of by using the rebar in the footing. If you do not see a ground wire, hire an electrician to make sure the home is grounded properly.

If you find the grounding rod, make sure the ground wire actually connects to the grounding rod. Sometimes the wire has been disconnected and is hanging loose. If it is connected, make sure it is connected with the correct clamp. It should not be connected with a hose clamp or a clamp that is made for indoor use only.

The ground rod should be driven at least six to eight feet into the ground. It should be copper-clad or galvanized. If you find an old galvanized pipe, check it to see if the connectors are rusted. If they are, it will make for a bad link to the ground wire. The ground rod should not be metal plumbing pipe or a painted pipe.

The grounding can also take place by hooking the grounding

wire to a water pipe. It should be hooked to the inlet water pipe that runs by the water meter. It should also be connected to the pipe using a "clamp on." If it is clamped to the pipe on the inside, it must have a jumper cable that circles the meter to the street side of the pipe. You should inspect the connection closely. It may be loose. It may be loosened by a previous homeowner who did not know what the connection was for. If the connection is loose, it needs to be tightened with a screwdriver.

You also need to make sure the water pipe is functioning. If a new water pipe has been installed, the ground wire should be moved to the new pipe. Also, if the pipe is plastic, polyvinyl chloride (PVC) or acrylonitrile-butadiene-styrene (ABS), it will do no good to have the grounding wire hooked up to it. Many homes that receive their water from a well have plastic water pipes.

POTENTIAL PROBLEMS/VIOLATIONS

Knob and tube wiring was installed in homes from the 1920s to the 1950s. Knob and tube wiring used single conductors that usually ran along side floor joists or rafters. The wiring was connected to a ceramic knob so that the wire itself never touched the wood. The wires went through the wood (the floor joists or rafters) in ceramic tubes. This kept it away from the wood.

You will not be able to see what type of wiring is behind the home's walls but you should be able to find some wiring in the basement (if it is unfinished) or in the attic. Knob and tube wiring is considered to be safe as long as it is in good condition and has not been changed in any way. If there are problems, or if you are concerned because you are dealing with an older home, consult an electrician.

In the basement, look for common electrical violations. Make sure there are no exposed wires or wires that have been openly spliced. Make sure there are no open junction boxes. If you have doubts about the wiring, ask the owner for a statement that certifies the wiring is up to codes and is safe.

Outside the home, check any outside poles or fountains have an underground wire running to them. If the wires are visible, check them to see if they are made to be outside. Often homeowners will use wiring that should only be used inside the home. If it was not specifically made to stand up to the elements and the soil, the wire will wear down and eventually malfunction. Check the lamp to make sure it works. If it does not, try a new light bulb. It could also be a problem with the switch, but be aware the wiring could be at fault.

Check all the outlets on the outside of the home. Make sure they work correctly. Also, check each of them to make sure they have covers over the plugs. Covers are needed to protect the outlet from water running inside them.

Inside the home, make sure all the electric outlets have covers. Also, make sure there are no extension cords running through walls. This is a clear violation. Extension cords are an indication that something is amiss. If power is needed, it should be supplied directly from a receptacle. If there is not one nearby, the wiring should be updated so that there is.

Any type of electrical problem or violation should be taken seriously because it could lead to a fire. Make sure all the electrical wiring and its accessories are as they need to be. Do not be afraid to hire an electrician if you need help or if you do not feel comfortable about anything. When dealing with electricity, it is always better to be safe than sorry.

House Inspection Tip #6

Check every outlet in the house. To do this, you can buy a handheld
tester at a hardware store. Make sure that all outlets are working
and make sure that there are enough outlets available for your
every day needs.

7

PLUMBING & SEPTIC

Plumbing and septic systems can cause major damage if something goes wrong with them. They can also be expensive to repair. Make sure you check out the plumbing and septic thoroughly during the inspection and that you continue to keep up with it while you are living in the home. Don't forget to see the appendices and the companion CD-ROM for sample checklists and forms you can use to keep track of all your findings when inspecting a home.

PLUMBING EQUIPMENT

Plumbing systems in homes are quite elaborate. The equipment involved includes fixtures, drainage system, waste-disposal system, vent stack, fresh-air vent, septic system, plumbing wall hatch, water supply pipes, drainage pipes, and distribution pipes. The plumbing equipment may also include the well-pumping system (piston pump/jet pump/submersible pump), storage tanks, and pressure switch and gauges.

PLUMBING OVERVIEW

Home plumbing made up of a source where water is drawn

from, piping that distributes the water, fixtures that produce the water, drainage piping, and a system that gets rid of waste. Most plumbing is not visible. It is important for you to inspect the parts that you can see. What you find there will let you know the condition of the plumbing.

Depending on where the house is located, the water is either supplied by a local water or utility company or by a pumping system that is hooked into a well. If the house has public water, the delivery system is pipe lines laid near the street. There is a shutoff valve at or near the property line that can be shut down if the water bill is not paid. From the shutoff valve, the pipe that brings the water to the house is called the house service main. If something happens to this pipe, it is the home owner's responsibility to get it fixed.

The water supply to an entire house can be turned off by an underground valve usually located near the water meter on the service main which branches to various parts of the house. One pipe takes water to the hot water heater, which can either be alone or part of the heating system. Pipes running from the hot water heater throughout the house should not be closer than six inches to the cold water pipes to avoid warming them.

Faucets and shower heads are the plumbing fixtures that deliver water for use. The drainage system is made up of three parts: trap, drain pipe, and vent. The trap is located just beneath the sink. As we discussed in Chapters 3 and 4, the traps can either be "P" traps or "S" traps. There should always be a small amount of water in the bottom of the trap. This water serves to form a seal so that sewer gases do not back through the drain and erupt from the sink.

From the trap, the waste water travels through the drain and out into a sewer or some type of sewage disposal. The drains need to be tilted slightly downward because the waste is removed by gravity. There is no pressure moving the water along like there is when the water is delivered to the fixtures. This is why the pipes draining the water are much wider in diameter than the pipes delivering the water.

Some municipalities require all homes to have a trap located near the foundation to stop sewer gases from backing into any part of the home. If there is a house trap, there should also be a fresh-air pipe linked into the main drain. The fresh-air pipe is on the outside of the home. It should be covered with a plate that has holes in it so that the air can flow through it, and it will not become clogged. If the pipe is standing alone, the end of it should have an additional pipe that it rounded and curved downward, referred to as a "gooseneck" cover.

Venting allows gases to pass out of the system into the air and also helps to even out the air pressure by allowing air to flow in and out of the drainpipes. Venting stops the water in the traps from being siphoned out. If the air pressure is uneven, water is siphoned away from the traps. Vents are located near the traps under each of the fixtures. There is also a vent that runs up to the roof. This pipe is visible and should always be kept free of clogs or other obstructions. This pipe is called the "vent stack" and it serves only to vent the drain lines. "Vent stacks" do not carry any incoming water or outgoing waste.

Waste produced in a house passes through a pipe and into either a sewer or into a septic tank or cesspool. Residential neighborhoods that are hooked up to public sewer have waste going into a sewer and on to a waste treatment plant. Sewers are easy maintenance.

In fact, there may be many years that pass without your giving the waste system any thought other than to pay the bill.

On the other hand, septic tanks need to be replaced occasionally and cleaned every two or three years. However, you do not have to pay a monthly fee to use the septic tank as you do with the sewer. You own the tank and you can use it free of charge.

It is impossible to tell whether a house has a sewer or if it has a septic tank. The pipes look the same. Most municipalities force homeowners to connect to a sewer system if the system runs by the house. However, not all require a hookup, and some people decide they do not want to tie into the sewer. While this occurrence may be rare, it does happen. Therefore, do not assume a house is hooked-up to a public sewer just because you know the sewer runs past the house. If you have a question, you should be able to get in touch with the local agency that handles the sewer and ask them if the house is hooked into the sewer system.

SEPTIC OVERVIEW

A septic tank is a large container that sits below the ground and takes in waste from the house. The container is watertight and usually made of concrete, but it could be made of fiberglass or steel. Raw sewage travels through the drains and empties into the septic tank. Bacteria then break down the waste, and the effluence that is liquid rises to the top. Pipes going from the septic tank allow the broken down waste to pass out of the tank and into the ground. The place where the waste seeps out is called a leach field. The size of the leach field should be determined by how fast the ground can absorb the waste. If there is not enough room for a sufficient leach field, a seepage pit may be used in conjunction with it.

A percolation test needs to be done to determine how large the leach field should be. A percolation test determines the soil's ability to absorb water. The percolation should not be done during a dry spell because absorption will be slower after the dry spell ends. If the soil cannot absorb the waste, the entire septic system will fail within 10 years when it should last from 20 to 50 years.

To check for a malfunctioning septic system, look around the area of the septic tank. Since problems show up around the leach field and not directly over the septic tank, be sure to inspect a wide area. Check for unusual wet spots or patches of grass that are much more lush and green than the rest of the lawn. When the leach field becomes overtaxed, waste begins to build up at the surface of the ground. The waste is a great fertilizer and that is why grass grows lush and green near the septic tank. Also, sniff around the entire area because the first indication you will have that a septic system is not working correctly is the foul smell it produces.

A leach field needs space in the soil that can absorb the waste that enters the septic system. Over time, these spaces fill-in so that waste begins to surface, requiring a new leach field to be installed. When you are inspecting the home, make sure there will be enough room to put in an additional leach field if the need arises. It will become a major problem for you if you need a new leach field at some point in the future and you have no place to put it.

A septic tank needs to be cleaned regularly, the schedule depending on its size and the number of people occupying the house. For example, 1,500-gallon tank serving three people needs to be cleaned every five or six years, as would a 2,000-gallon tank serving four people. If the septic tank is not cleaned, sludge will build up and cause all the waste to go into the leaching field instead of the septic tank. This will cause the spaces in the leach field to fill quickly or it could clog the spaces in the leaching field pipes, requiring the leach field to need to be replaced. Problems can be stopped before they starts simply by cleaning and checking the septic tank every two to four years.

There are ways of extending the life of a septic tank and leaching field. Obviously, the fewer people who live in a house, the longer the septic tank will last. You can have water from the washing machine and other such fixtures running into a dry well or a septic pit that is separate from the leaching field.

Do not buy into advertising for products that claim to cut down on the need to clean the septic tank by improving bacterial activity. There will always be a sludge build-up that needs to be cleaned away. The product you pour down the drain to help the septic system may actually hurt it by stopping the bacteria from working.

If the home you are inspecting has a grease trap in the waste disposal system, it will help extend the life of the septic system. Grease can get into the tank and the leaching field where it will make it less able to absorb the waste. The grease could also adversely affect the way the bacteria works inside the septic tank. A grease trap will cut down on and nearly eliminate these types of problems. Be aware that the trap will need to be cleaned regularly to work well.

Rainwater should not enter the septic tank because great amounts of water will eventually make the entire system malfunction.

Excess water can cause the tank to overflow and eventually cause the leach field spaces to be clogged.

Recharge wastes from a properly operating water softener will not harm septic tank action, but the additional water must be treated and disposed of by the drain field. If the softener recharge overloads the sewage system, this waste water can be discharged to the ground surface since it contains no pathogens. But it must be discharged in a location where it will not be a nuisance or damage valuable grass or plants.

Ask when the septic tank was cleaned. It should not have been longer than four years. If the owner gives you permission, you can check the system yourself by running water down the tub for about an hour. If the faucet is turned all the way on, this should send enough water into the septic system to cause any problems that might exist to surface. Do not run water for any length of time if your water comes from a well as doing so will burn out the motor.

Some septic systems require pumps to send the waste into the leaching field. The pumps are usually needed when the leaching field is uphill from the house. In this case, there will be a septic tank that will process the waste and then the effluence will pass into the second tank that has the pump. The pump will then send the effluence from the tank out into the leaching field. Newer pumping tanks will have a lid in the ground so that they are easily accessible. Older tanks were completely buried underground. Take note whether you see a lid. If the pump stops working, the effluence will rise to the top of the tank and sound an alarm. There should be a switch you can use to test the alarm. Throw the switch to "test" or "alarm" and then wait. If it is working, you should see a red light begin flashing and hear an alarm sound.

If it is unplugged, plug it in and then test the alarm. If the alarm is not working, you will have no way of knowing whether the pump is working.

Some local governments require that a pumping system consist of two pumps. This allows one pump to continue to pump the waste while the other pump is being repaired so that water can continue to be used in the house.

You may also run across a septic system that uses a chlorination system. These systems are necessary when the house is too close to a creek or the land is too low for a septic tank. Chlorination systems have lids that stick up out of the ground. The lids will probably be round and in a row. The chlorination system is like a mini water treatment plant. It takes the waste in, treats it with massive amounts of chlorination and then sends it out to a nearby creek. Do not try to test anything with this type of system. Inquire whether it is under warranty and who is used to perform the maintenance on it.

PLUMBING INSIDE THE HOME

To recap chapters three and four that went into detail about how to inspect the sinks, drains, and faucets in the home:

- Make sure all the fixtures work and that the water flow is good.

- Be sure the drains work correctly and that they do not leak.

- Check for loose sinks or bowls.

- Make sure all the toilets in the house operate correctly and that they do not have any leaks either.

- Look for signs of past leaking that has caused damage around sinks, bowls, pipes, or drains.

- Double check all the fixtures, pipes, and drains.

Problems with the pipes bringing water to the fixtures are usually the cause of water not flowing well. Bad water pressure is usually caused by a buildup of minerals in the pipes, corrosion, or a kink in the pipe. The flow of water will only be as good as the worst section of pipe it travels through.

Water supply pipes can be either brass, copper, or galvanized iron. To determine which you have, galvanized iron and brass pipes have threaded joints while copper pipes have soldered joints. You can use a magnet to detect galvanized iron since a magnet will not attach to brass. The pipe should be all of one type and not a combination. Mixing pipes together can lead to accelerated corrosion which causes leaks. If you see joined pipes that are different, inspect them closely for leakage. If there is no problem, expect one in the near future.

You should locate the water pipe that is running into the home. It will be near the foundation of the house and usually has a water meter near it. This pipe is called the inlet service pipe because it brings water into the house. It is normally made of brass, copper, or galvanized iron. Some older homes used lead piping. You can tell if the pipe is lead or not by scratching it gently. If it is lead the surface will be fairly soft and will reveal a silver-gray area where it was scratched. Lead can be harmful to humans (especially children and pregnant women). If you discover lead pipes, have the water tested for lead content. Most health departments will perform this test for free. If the water is found to be too high in lead, the owner will have to pay for it to be replaced.

If the flow of water is still bad after all the pipes have been found to be in good shape and all the same kind of pipe, there has to be a problem with the inlet pipe or with the pressure from the main pipe outside the home. The inlet pipe should last about 40 years but it will eventually wear out and begin to leak. Replacement can be costly but it is necessary.

If the water is supplied by a utility company and no other troubled spots were found, the problem probably is the water pressure out at the street. The pressure is not enough to keep up with the demand of all the houses on the street. To solve this problem, you can install a storage tank to collect water and hold it until it is needed. When you need the water, you will draw from your own holding tank rather than the outside pipe that has insufficient pressure. The tank will replace the used water when there are no fixtures running water in the home. Such a tank may already be present in the home you are inspecting. If so, take note of it.

If the house is more rural, a well may supply the water. There are three different types of wells: drilled, driven, and dug. Dug wells are rare but you may encounter one. Usually these types of wells are not deep in the ground.

The condition of your well and its closeness to contamination sources determine the risk it poses to the groundwater. For example, a cracked well casing allows bacteria, nitrates, oil, and pesticides to enter the well more easily. A spill of pesticides being mixed and loaded right near the well could result in the contamination of the groundwater. Preventing groundwater contamination is very important. Once the groundwater supplying your well is contaminated, it is nearly impossible to clean up. The only options for new drinking water would be to treat the water, drill a new well, or get water from another source. These options would be expensive and inconvenient. A contaminated well may also affect your neighbors' water source, posing a serious threat to their health. Your best option is to prevent groundwater contamination.

To be safe, you should have the well water tested for germs every year and for chemicals every two or three years. Do not be afraid to have it tested at anytime if you suspect that something is wrong with the well or the water. You could also install an ultraviolet (UV) filter. UV filters, when working correctly, will kill any bacteria that pass through the inlet water pipe. The correct way to inspect the filter will be discussed later in this chapter.

The water is taken from the well and sent into the water pipes running into the house by a well pump that should push the water hard enough past resistance in the pipes, providing sufficient flow at the water fixtures.

The three types of well pumps are submersible, jet, and piston. While all three pumps can be used for shallow or deep wells, the submersible pump is usually the pump of choice for deep wells. The submersible pump is the only pump that actually sits in the water. The other two pumps suck the water out of the well. That is why the submersible pump is the logical choice for deep wells — water in deep wells may be too difficult for a pump to suck out.

The submersible pump is made so that the electric motor and the pump can run under water. The water is drawn into the pump through screens and then sent up through one pipe into a storage tank that is usually located in the lowest level of the home. If the well has a submersible pump, make sure there is a lightning arrestor connected to the motor. This is important because the motor sits in water and is susceptible to lightning strikes. Submersible pumps are generally reliable and noise free. However, if a submersible pump does break, the entire apparatus will have to be pulled out of the well.

Most likely you will not run into a piston pump unless you are looking at an old home where the well has not been updated. The piston pump is basically a hand pump with a motor. A piston pump alternates between sucking the water from the well and spitting it out. If the well is shallow, the entire unit will be above ground. This includes the motor and the piston. If the well is deeper, the motor will be above ground but the piston will be under the ground in the well. You should see that the motor and the piston are connected by a belt and pulley. Make sure the belt is tight enough and look for any spots that are worn. Be sure to check for signs of leaking around the piston rod and the casing joints.

A jet pump can be used for shallow or deep wells. The motor spins a centrifugal pump that draws water up into the jet assembly. The water is circulated and some of it goes up and out of the pump to the house while the rest is re-circulated so that the suction is able to continue to draw even more water up into the pump. Jet pumps need to be replaced if they are frozen.

There are accessories that need to go along with a well for it to work. When the water leaves the well, it goes to a storage tank to regulate water pressure. It may be in the lowest level of the house or it could be in a pump house. A tank that is working correctly should have a constant reserve of water available whenever it is needed by a fixture in the house.

The storage tank has to have some air in it to provide pressure. If the tank does not have a diaphragm to provide pressure, over time or because of a leak, air decreases and the tank becomes waterlogged. The effect is the same as there being no tank at all. The pump must start and stop every time there is a need for water at one of the fixtures in the home. If the pump is a jet or a piston type pump, you will hear the pump clicking on and off every time there is a need for water. If it is a submersible pump, you can tell if it is waterlogged by looking at the pressure switch. It will be clicking on and off. If allowed to continue, the pump will burn out. You can also check the pressure gauge and see if it is bouncing between high and low pressure limits. A waterlogged tank needs to be drained and have air injected back into it or to be replaced with a tank that has a diaphragm in it to separate the air and water. The problem is easy to fix but you should still take note if you find a waterlogged tank in the house you are inspecting.

Most local governments require that the tank be insulated so that condensation does not build up on it during the summer. Check the tank to make sure it is not rusted or showing other signs of deterioration. The tank may need to be replaced, or it may need to be scraped down, repainted, and then insulated again.

A pressure switch and gauge must be on every system. The switch automatically clicks on and off when the gauge reaches certain predetermined pressures. The normal pressure range is usually between 20 pounds per square inch (PSI) and 40 PSI, 30 and 50 PSI, or sometimes 40 and 60 PSI. Anytime the PSI is over

65 you should contact a professional to look at the pump. The abnormal pressure may be caused by a bad pressure switch.

You can check the switch by running the water from a faucet. With the water still running, look at the pressure gauge as it goes down from the water running out of the tank. Once the gauge reaches the low limit, the pump should turn off. Turn the water off at the faucet and watch while the pressure builds back up as the water is pumped into the tank. The switch should click back off when the pressure reaches the upper limit. If the pump does not stop or stops at too high a pressure, you know there is a problem. Obviously if the gauge is completely broken, the test cannot be run and the gauge needs to be replaced.

Make sure there is a relief valve on the tank or pipes to ensure that the excess pressure is relieved if the switch does not turn the pump off when it should. Also, check the pressure gauge to make sure the tank holds the pressure while there is no water being used and the pump is not operating. If the pressure drops, you know there is a leak. If you found no leaks when inspecting the pipes, you can assume the leak is somewhere between the tank and the well.

Sometimes you will find a UV filter beside the storage tank. The filter will be stainless steel with a light attached to it. Make sure the filter is firmly attached to the wall. It should be plumbed into the main water line after the storage tank and any other water treatment systems such as water softeners or iron removers. The UV filter should be located before the main line branches off into other lines that will carry the water throughout the house. Peek through the hole to make sure the light is on. Also, look for a tag somewhere that will tell you when the bulb was last changed or when it will need to be changed. Most bulbs are good for about 14 months.

The UV filter will not work if the light cannot touch all the water that is coming into the house. Therefore, the water cannot have any debris floating in it. To stop the debris, you may find a cartridge filter that is installed above the UV filter. If you can, check to make sure the cartridge is present.

Another potential problem could be too much iron in the water. You will not know if the water has too much iron but a softener may be installed to help alleviate this problem. If there is a water softener, make sure it is not set to "bypass." Also make sure the cartridge filter is not set to "bypass" either. If the cartridge and water softener are not on, the UV filter will not work properly. Despite the presence of a UV filter, water from a well should always be tested before anyone new moves into a house.

Finally, if you are not sure how well the water is flowing through your pipes, you can perform a water pressure test. This test is easily performed by attaching a water pressure gauge to an outside hose bib. Technically you can hook the pressure gauge onto a faucet in the house but faucets could have aerators that cause the gauge to measure incorrectly. Therefore, it is best to hook the gauge onto a hose bib. Once it is hooked on, turn the water on. Depending on where the house is located, the highest the pressure should read is around 70 or 80 PSI. To avoid water pressure problems, the PSI should be above 30.

If you are measuring the water pressure where the water is provided by a utility company, the pressure should remain constant. However, if the water is coming from a well, the pressure will fluctuate by 20 PSI depending on when you perform the test because of the gauge's being located on the storage tank (as was already explained). If the house does have water from a well, you will only need to perform the water pressure test if the gauge on the storage tank is missing or broken. Otherwise, the pressure will be displayed on the gauge that you looked at before. You can adjust the gauge to turn on and off at different PSI levels. If you are inspecting the home for someone else, do not adjust the gauge on your own. The future owner should have a plumber adjust it because the air in the tank will have to be adjusted as well.

DRAINAGE PIPES

Waste from the sinks and the toilet runs from the fixtures down the drainage pipes and into the sewer or the septic tank. You will only be able to see the part of the drainage pipe that is in the basement. If the house does not have a basement and is built on the ground level or if the basement is finished, you will not be able to inspect the pipes at all because they will be hidden. Therefore, you will not be able to inspect these pipes either.

The drainage pipes can be made of copper, lead, plastic, cast iron, or galvanized iron. The pipes can be made of any of these types and they can be mixed and matched. You do not have to worry about the copper and iron reacting negatively when placed together as you did with the water distribution pipes.

The waste leaves through the pipes by the force of gravity. This means that the main drain must gradually slope downward until it reaches the sewer or the septic tank. Look closely at the pipe and make sure there are no points that are lower than the rest. If there is, it will cause a problem sooner or later. Eventually solid waste will settle in that section of the pipe and cause a blockage to occur. A pipe like this is a violation and must be fixed. Also, while looking at the drainage pipes, check for any evidence of past problems with the pipes. The evidence may be patched sections of the pipe or signs of leakage.

Some finished basements have bathrooms in them. These bathrooms will have waste that needs to be drained but cannot be carried away by gravity because the fixtures are located below the drainage pipes. The waste is able get into the main drainage pipe with the help of a sewer ejector tank. This tank can usually be found in the part of the basement that is not finished. The tank will be installed below the floor. The only parts that will be visible to you will be the vent pipes and the top cover. The top cover should be firmly fastened to the tank, and there should be enough seals around where the pipes run from the tank. The cover also needs to have a gasket. On the discharge line you should be able to find two valves: a check valve and a gate valve. The entire ejector pump is run by a float switch. One way to see whether the pump works correctly is to flush the toilet and then run the water in the bathroom sink. Wait until the pump turns on and make sure it pumps the water out into the drain pipe.

Sometimes the house drain is located beneath the basement floor or slab. If you wish to connect any new fixtures to the drain (for example: installing a bathroom in the basement), you will have to break up certain sections of the floor. When you install the new drain lines, you should make sure the fixtures are close to the drain lines that are already there to reduce the cost and effort of installation.

SUPPLY PIPES

An earlier section in this chapter, "Plumbing Inside the Home," discussed supply pipes. You need to make sure they are working correctly and that they do not have any of the defects mentioned earlier in the chapter. Watch for corroding pipes that will eventually leak. Pipes made by linking various kinds of material will lead to early corrosion problems. Also, watch for lead pipes that could lead to health problems, especially for children. Test the water to make sure it has no lead in it. You should also test the water periodically to make sure it is safe to drink.

Copper pipes have a tendency to spring tiny leaks. Sometimes a leak will result in a spray of water coming out of the pipe, and other times it will show itself as a small drip of water that runs along the pipe. If the water inside the pipe freezes, it will expand the pipe. Copper will not return to its original state once it has been stretched. Therefore, once the water in the pipe has frozen and expanded the copper, you will not be able to fit any copper fitting over the pipe. Also, if the water contains a small amount of acid, the pipe will erode from the inside out. You may know if this happening if you see greenish-blue stains in your sinks and tub.

You may find red or yellow brass pipes in the house, which are easy to distinguish by their color (red-brass is not exactly red but more of a pale brown). Yellow-brass usually lasts about 40 years. It corrodes easily and allows zinc to pass out of the brass and into the water. Red-brass pipes can last about 70 years. The weakest point of the brass pipes is the threaded joints. The weak joints can rupture if any type of pressure is applied to them. Look for mineral deposits that have become encrusted around the joints, a sure sign of weak joints. If you find them, plan on replacing or at least repairing those sections of the pipes.

As with the other types of pipes, you should look along the entire brass pipe for signs of leaking. Small pinhole leaks are common in brass pipes. They are caused by the water drawing the zinc out of the pipes. You may see small water droplets on the pipes. Sometimes the water evaporates before it becomes a drop but it will leave behind a whitish stain around the leak. Sometimes deposits will seal the holes and solve the problem, but eventually the hole will grow larger. If you see any sign of a leaking pipe, plan on replacing the pipes in the near future.

Plastic pipe, or CPVC, is another type you may find for your water supply pipes. These pipes are pale colored. Some plastic pipes are made from polyvinyl chloride (PVC) that is white. These pipes usually do not run throughout the home but they may be used to bring water into the home from the city supply or a well. All plastic pipes may be a problem because they crack easily, for instance, during a freeze. Water expands, splitting the plastic pipes into long sections. Also, check the fitting between the male and female parts. Plastic pipes have a tendency to leak at the fittings.

You need to be careful of metal pipes running into CPVC. If a male metal pipe is screwed into a female CPVC, the plastic pipe will crack easily. You probably will not be able to see the crack with your eyes. Look out for a small, slow drip or what is known as water tracking. Look for rust stains that are reddish in color. You may also see a small puddle of water or a water stain on the floor below the pipe.

One kind of pipe that has been banned in new constructions is called PB. It is a flexible, gray pipe that has had major problems with its fittings. If you see this pipe, make sure it is not leaking at the ring joints and that it is not clamped down with hose clamps.

The clamps cannot be sharp or they will cut into the PB and cause it to leak. The PB should not be glued down either.

If you see galvanized pipe, be aware that this kind of pipe sometimes rusts on the inside but is not visible from the outside. The rust can become so bad that it cuts off the water supply. More commonly it will cause the water flow to decrease, dropping the water pressure in the house. The rust could also break away and get stuck in different places including washer screens and toilet refill valves.

There are a number of problems that can arise with pipe fittings. Fittings can often break during installation or can spring a leak afterwards. Watch for patches on fittings because they signal that there is leak and the owner tried to stop the leak rather than replace the fitting.

You need make sure the main water line has a shutoff valve. Every house is required to have one. The shutoff valve can stop the water supply for the entire house. You may even see two valves, one on each side of the water meter. Use caution when checking to see if the valve works. It may break when you check it and stay in the off or on position. You may choose not to check whether it is functional, but you should make sure that there is a main shutoff valve.

Finally, while you are checking the shutoff valve, be sure to look for an anti-flowback device or a "check" valve. These devices stop water from one house from flowing back into the water supply for all the other houses around it. Without being stopped, the water in one house could contaminate the water supply for all the other houses in the area.

House Inspection Tip #7

Be sure you check the plumbing of the house before you buy it.
Make note of any leaks you may find. Run the water to see if it is
clear or if it produces a discharge.

8

THE ATTIC

It is important that you inspect the attic. There are four basic things you want to check in the attic: potential roof leaks, physical state of the rafters and sheathing, insulation, and condition of any equipment in the attic. However, you also need to look out for potential hazards and violations, too. You may want to wait to inspect the attic until after you perform an outside inspection of the roof. That way you can note potential roof problems on the exterior and then check to see if there is a leak on the inside.

The attic can be a dangerous place to inspect. There are certain tools and devices you will want to bring with you to help with the attic inspection. If the attic is only accessible through a hole (known as a scuttle hole) you will want to bring along a ladder to help you get into the attic. You will also want two flashlights, plywood boards, protective glasses, and possibly a hard hat. Don't forget to see the appendices and the companion CD-ROM for sample checklists and forms you can use to keep track of all your findings when inspecting a home.

ENTERING THE ATTIC

There are several possibilities for entry into the attic. You may be lucky enough to have a stairway or a pull-down ladder, but you may well only have a little hole that you have to climb up through. This hole could be located in a closet or anywhere. The first thing you may have to do is find the opening and then figure out a way to get up through it. After you locate the access point, you will want to use a ladder, preferably a folding ladder, to get up into the attic.

If the point of entry is through a scuttle hole, you will have to remove the panel that covers the hole. To do this, you should carefully push up on the panel and then move it to one side. Use caution while doing this because you never know what might fall out as you shift the panel. Be sure to wear a pair of protective glasses because of any particles that might fall down onto your face.

Look around the attic before climbing into it. Shine a flashlight and look for possible hazards such as wires or anything else you might trip over. If the attic does not have a floor, you will probably want to lay boards of plywood or planks down across the ceiling joists so that you do not step on the ceiling and break through it. You will also want to place one flashlight to provide light to the entire attic. You should have a second flashlight that you carry to focus on specific locations. Be careful of nails that are poking down into the attic through the sheathing. You do not want a rusty nail – or any nail – to poke through your head. You may want to wear a hard hat so that you do not have to worry about the nails.

TYPES OF ATTICS

Ironically, if you are able to walk around in the attic, it is a "full" attic. Sometimes these attics have floors but do not have a finished ceiling or finished walls. You may also find partition walls that form rooms that are finished including the ceilings. Stairs usually provide access to full attics.

If you have to crouch over or crawl into the attic, it is known as a "crawl" attic. This type of attic has to be left unfinished because of the amount of space between the roof and the floor of the attic. Crawl attics rarely have floors. This means that you will be able to see the ceiling joists below. If you did not bring along plywood to walk or crawl on, be sure you only walk or crawl on the joists. If you place any kind of real weight on the ceiling, you will break right through into the room below. Crawl attics are usually only accessible with a pull-down ladder or through a scuttle hole.

INSULATION

Insulation is an important part of any home where temperatures are extreme. It will keep the heat in your house during the winter and keep it out during the summer. The amount of insulation, along with the rating, depends on where the house is located. The effectiveness of the insulation is usually measured by the R-number. The higher the R-number, the more effective the insulation will be. You can add R-numbered insulation together so that insulation with an R-number of 11 can be added to insulation rated R-13 to provide insulation of R-24.

Insulation comes in many different materials and forms. The three most widely used types are loose-fill, flexible, and rigid. Loose-fill insulation can be made of a variety of different materials. Some of the common materials are rock wool, wood shavings, sawdust, glass fibers, or vermiculite. It can come in bales or bags and can be installed by hand, poured, or blown.

Loose-fill is perfect for walls or in attics where there is a floor covering. It is not recommended for any place that is not covered because it is loose.

Flexible insulation is made in either batts or blankets. It consists of a fibrous material like cotton or rock wool. Chemicals are added to the insulation materials so that they are fire-proof and resistant to decay. Batts come in pre-cut sections while bales are continuous rolls. They each come in two widths so that they can fit between joist and studs that are spaced either 16 or 24 inches apart.

Rigid insulation is usually made of urethane, polystyrene bead board, extruded polystyrene, or wood fiberboard. It is made in widths of 24 or 48 inches and is usually not fire proof. This type of insulation should be covered with gypsum wallboard that is at least a half inch thick to make the insulation fire resistant. Rigid insulation is often used to back aluminum and vinyl siding on the outside of the home. It is also used for masonry walls. Rigid insulation is not used in attics.

Insulation should be located between floor joists, not on the underside of the roof. It should also have a vapor barrier that is facing the ceiling of the room below to stop condensation from collecting in the insulation, reducing its effectiveness. The vapor barrier may be a plastic sheet, an asphalt-impregnated paper, or aluminum foil. If the vapor barrier is positioned wrong and enough condensation builds up, the paint of the walls and ceiling below may begin to peel.

Check in the attic for air-conditioning or heating ducts. They should be insulated. If there is no insulation on the outside of the ducts, check to see if the insulation is on the inside. To do this, you can simply knock on the duct with your flashlight. If it makes a dull thud, there is insulation inside. If it sounds hollow, there is no insulation. You will need to wrap three inches of insulation around the duct. You will need to cover the insulation with a vapor barrier if the duct is for an air-conditioner to stop condensation from building up.

If the house is located in a colder climate and the furnace is in the attic, there needs to be insulation between the roof rafters as well as between the floor joists. The insulation between the roof rafters should not be flush against the roof. There should be a small amount of air space between the insulation and the roof. The space that is left, along with the insulation, will help keep the deck of the roof cool. If the roof warms up too much, it will melt the bottom layer of snow on the roof and this could lead to an ice dam forming. Ice dams can cause melting snow to back-up and leak into the house. This will be covered more in Chapter 14.

VENTS/VENTILATION

It is important to have proper ventilation in the attic to help get rid of extra moisture that may build up and to help keep the attic from overheating in the summer. Small to moderate amounts of moisture will find its way to the attic from the kitchen and the bathroom(s). Any excessive moisture that builds up can cause problems in the home. These problems include peeling paint in the rooms below the attic, water streaks on the walls, and could even result in the wood framing rotting.

When you are in the attic, make sure all the vents are open and unblocked. Some of the vents may have been closed to stop the heat from escaping and keep the cold air from coming in during the cold months. As long as the attic is properly insulated, there will not be enough heat escaping through the vent openings to make a difference. It is much more important to make sure that the moisture in the attic is allowed to escape from the house.

If you are looking at the attic during the warm months, check the sheathing near the nails. If you see rust in the sheathing, you know that there is probably a problem with ventilation. In the cold months, you can see if the nails poking through the sheathing are covered with frost. If they are, there is not enough ventilation. When it warms up, the frost will melt and drip down onto the insulation leaving little round water stains.

It is not difficult to fix an improperly ventilated attic. If there are preexisting vents in the attic, you may just have to open them wider. If not, you may need to install additional vents. Consult a professional to determine exactly how many vents you will need.

Another solution to attic ventilation problems is to install a power ventilator, which is usually controlled by a thermostat. When the attic reaches a certain temperature, the power ventilator will kick on and pull the out air of the attic, particularly useful during the summer months, especially if the house has a cooling system. By sucking the hot air out of the attic, the power ventilator will cut down on the energy needed to cool the home. You should notice the power ventilator running most of the time in the summer. If it does not, there is either something wrong with it, or the thermostat is set at the wrong temperature. If it is not running when you inspect the attic, lower the thermostat until it is low enough to trigger the operation of the fan.

ROOF CRACKS/LEAKS

Possibly the most important job you will have while inspecting the attic is looking for signs of leaks from the roof. You should look on the underside of the roof, at the sheathing, and at the rafters for dark stains on the wood. If it happens to be raining while you are inspecting the attic, you might be able to see a leak as it occurs. Be careful not to mistake condensation from improper ventilation as a roof leak.

While checking for leaks, pay particular attention to the spots around any chimneys or smokestacks that might run up through the roof. Leaks often occur where the chimney or smokestack actually meets the roof. If you find a leak at one of the joints between chimney and roof or smokestack and roof, do not be overly concerned. This type of leak is usually easy to fix. It can simply be resealed with asphalt cement.

FIRE HAZARDS

You need to pay particular attention if the house you are inspecting has a prefabricated chimney. The joint where the chimney meets the attic floor needs to be inspected closely. There should be at least two inches between the chimney and the wood framing beside it. This is an important code because although wood does not normally ignite until it reaches at least 400°F; it can catch fire at about 200° if it has been exposed to 150 degrees or higher for a long period. However, the gap between the prefabricated chimney and the wood frame can also pose a problem. The chimney usually runs from the furnace/boiler all the way up through the attic. If a fire starts in the furnace/boiler, the space will act as a flue and pull the flames right up to the attic. Once the flames are in the attic, the house will quickly be consumed in flames. This can be easily avoided by fire-stopping the gap with a material that is not combustible.

If the house you are inspecting has a wood stove or a fireplace, you need to find where the chimney runs up through the attic. Check the joints to see if there is any sign of soot or creosote. Creosote buildup is the number one cause for chimney fires. If you see buildup on the joints in the attic, it means the smoke from the fire is escaping from the chimney into the attic. This happens more often with chimneys that do not have lined flues. If you see soot or creosote on the joints, it is a fire hazard and must be repaired.

VIOLATIONS

When in the attic look for any wiring that is illegal. You can also check the backside of light fixtures that are in the ceiling and up into the attic. Look for bare wires or illegal wire splices. Make sure there are no junction boxes. There should not be any unconventional wiring such as permanently powering something with an extension cord. Consult Chapter 6 for more information on wiring and fixtures.

Make sure there are no vent stacks that stop in the attic. Vent stacks need to go all the way through the roof so that the sewer gases escape into the atmosphere. You also need to look at the ducts from the exhaust fans and air conditioners. The joints should be sealed. You may find that an exhaust fan stops once it reaches the attic, causing excess moisture and condensation. All ducts from exhaust fans should go above the roof line so that the exhaust travels into the air outside. Make sure you find all the necessary ducts from the exhaust fans because some or all of them may be hidden by the insulation.

CONCLUSION

There are three additional things you should check out while you are in the attic. If there is some type of equipment in the attic, you will need to check it. There should be a switched light around the equipment. If there is not, make a note of it. Sometimes you will find that the heat pump has been placed in the attic. This could cause a problem in the future. The heat pump could begin leaking without your knowing it resulting in the loss of the entire ceiling below it.

If there is an attic fan, you will need to inspect it as well. Before you enter the attic, see if the attic fan is running. Be careful if it is on while you are in the attic. Before you enter the attic, place your hand over an outlet on the floor below the attic if the fan is on. If you feel air on your hand, you know there is not proper ventilation for the air the fan is trying to push out of the attic. This is usually because the opening in the vent is too small for the fan, causing the pressure in the attic to build up decreasing its ability to work as well as it should. These fans are either controlled manually, by a timer, or by a thermostat. A manual switch is not as good as the other types of switches. If the attic fan has a manual switch, you may want to replace it with a timer or a thermostat.

Finally, you need to inspect the structure above the attic. Check the trusses and the rafters for any sign of damage including cracking and sagging. Make sure the rafters are not separating at the ridge. These problems are uncommon but if you find them, consult a professional. They indicate a major problem with the structure of the home. If the floor joists have been cut to make room for pull-down stairs or something else, make sure the cut ends have been correctly connected to a header. If the trusses have been used for roof framing, make sure no cords or webs have been taken out. If they have been, the ability of the truss to perform as it should has been compromised. Be sure to make a note of the problem.

9
HEATING & COOLING

Do not breeze past the heating and cooling systems in the home. They will be responsible for keeping you comfortable and, during certain times, keeping you alive. If either system breaks down, it will be expensive to fix and far more costly to replace. Heating and cooling systems are complicated so if you become confused or feel that you need help, do not hesitate to bring in a heating and cooling specialist to check over the systems.

Also, you need to make sure you know where the fuel storage tanks are located and be sure you take the time to inspect them.

Don't forget to see the appendices and the companion CD-ROM for sample checklists and forms you can use to keep track of all your findings when inspecting a home.

HEATING

Heat will be from either a central heating system or area heaters. With central heating the heat is generated from one source—usually a furnace or a boiler—and distributed to individual rooms and areas. There are three basic types of central heating: warm air, hot water, and steam. An area or space heater is used to heat a specific section of the house. Fireplaces and stoves also fall into this category. The major energy sources used for heating are electricity, gas, and oil.

Most homes in the United States are heated by central heating systems, which use a burner to convert gas or oil into heat. If the home uses electric heat, a resistance coil is used to change the electricity into heat.

A heat exchanger is either a furnace or a boiler. A furnace heats the air, and a boiler heats water. Both are referred to as furnaces. After being turned into steam, air, or hot water, it needs to be sent throughout the house to provide the heat. The distribution system is made up of ducts or pipes that are used to carry the steam, air, or hot water. After traveling through the ducts or pipes, the heat is sent into the rooms of the house through outlets known as registers or radiators. The entire system is controlled by automatic safety controls and temperature controls.

You will want to ask the age of the furnace or boiler. Obviously the older the heat exchanger, the more concern there should be about its operation and possible future repair needs. You will also want to check the duct work and the pipes.

If the heating system is forced air, it probably has duct work to distribute the heat throughout the house. You need to check to make sure the ducts are in good shape and that they are not damaged in any way. Also check each heat source and make sure it is delivering heat and that there is not a return vent within ten feet of a burner flame. Also, listen when the fan in the unit clicks on. If the ducts make popping noises, the fan is unable to pull in enough air and is sucking it from the ducts, meaning the entire system is unbalanced.

You also need to inspect the flue pipe. The flue is the round duct that travels from the heating unit up to and through the roof. It is sometimes connected to an older chimney. The flue pipe should be single walled and supported every three or four feet so that it does not fall apart. The sections of the pipe are connected by having a smaller end sliding into a larger end. They will disconnect fairly easily so make sure there are no pipes that have pulled loose and left a gap. If it is indeed single-walled, you need to make sure the pipe is not within six inches of anything flammable.

Check around the flue pipe where it runs into the chimney for rust and corrosion. If you find it, you will probably need to have a professional look at the pipe because it is difficult to inspect and needs a professional's expertise. You will also need to check the flue for holes or large cracks. These gaps will stop gases from traveling up the flue and may even allow carbon monoxide to enter the home. If there is a clean-out door in the bottom of the chimney, you need to make sure it is closed tightly so that carbon monoxide will not escape into the house.

Check to see if there is a second appliance vent running into the same chimney as the flue. Most of the time it is against code to have two different types of gasses venting through the same chimney. The most common violation you may see is the flue running into the chimney of a wood stove. You also need to look for vent openings that are no longer being used. These openings need to be sealed off permanently.

Have a professional check the duct work to see if it is electrically hot.

Any time you are inspecting a forced air heating or cooling system, you will need to take a look at the air filter. The filter should be located somewhere between the blower and the return-air duct on the furnace. It may be slid in horizontally or vertically depending on the manufacturer. Take the air filter out and try to look through it. Hold it in front of a light. If you cannot see through it, it needs to be replaced. A clogged filter reduces the ability of the system to blow air, causing the system to run longer to heat or cool the house. Make sure you replace the air filter correctly before you move on.

You also need to check the chimney and the flue for back drafting, which happens when gases, which should be exiting the house through the flue, go back into the house because of the conditions outside the home (natural causes) or because of humans. If there is a high degree of back drafting and the unit has a sealed flue, you will be able to see the flames inside the combustion chamber bend over and dance all around as the back draft occurs. You could also hold a mirror up to where you think the back draft might be happening. A back draft will cause moisture to collect on the mirror. Small pressure changes from exhaust fans, clothes dryers, and other mechanical systems can cause heating system vents and chimneys to back draft into the living space. Digital manometer testing of flues and combustion rooms for depressurization can reveal this troublesome issue. You could elect to buy a digital manometer that will test gas pressures for you or to have a professional check the back draft.

One major advantage of central heating is that it can be zoned to heat more or fewer rooms to save on heating and air conditioning costs because the parts of the house that are not being used at times can be set at a low temperature. For example, at night when everyone is sleeping, the temperatures in the part of the house that is vacant can be turned down. Zone heating is a separate distribution system for each zone in the home. If there is zone heating, the thermostats (temperature controls) should also have timers on them so you can program them to make certain parts of the home warmer or colder automatically according to your needs. If the thermostats have no timers, you want to consider changing them over.

Heating systems should have at least one shutoff switch, normally located somewhere near the furnace or boiler. The switch could also be located at the top of the stairs that lead down to where the heating system is located. The master switch should be used to shut down the boiler or furnace in cases of emergency and when the heating system needs to be serviced. While the switch is off, there will be no heat from the boiler of furnace.

Often a central heating system will not heat the house evenly. Some parts of the home will be too warm while other parts may be too cool. The larger the home, the more difficult it is to heat it evenly. The registers and radiators that are farther from the furnace or boiler have a more difficult time heating rooms than those that are closer. You can help alleviate this problem by using different techniques depending on what type of central heating system is in the home. You will need specific types of air valves for steam systems, dampers for warm air systems, and throttling valves for hot water systems. You need to live in the house for a while so that you can determine if the system needs to be more evenly balanced.

As we mentioned in Chapter 2, the placement of heating outlets in rooms is important. The registers or radiators should be located near a window so that the heat mixes with the cold air to eliminate cold spots in any room. If the outlets are not located on the exterior walls in the room, the heat may not be distributed evenly.

There are pluses and minuses to all types of heating systems. It is up to you how important the type of heating system is to your decision to buy a house.

HEATED AIR SYSTEMS

There are good and bad aspects to heating with warm air. A furnace heats the air and sends it through ducts into rooms through registers in the wall, floor, or through a ceiling diffuser. Warm air pushes the cold air out of the room through return ducts. The cooler air travels back to the furnace where it is heated and sent throughout the house again. If there are no return ducts for the cold air, the air will travel back to the furnace with the help of gravity. It will usually travel down the stairs to the first floor and then seep down to the furnace through grills located on the first floor. With no return ducts, closing room doors will cause the heating to be less efficient.

In older homes, cold air that the furnace pulls in to heat comes directly from the basement. This is not as efficient because the air is cold when the furnace pulls it in and therefore it requires energy to be heated. This method can also be dangerous if the air that is being pulled in is poisonous. If the chimney becomes clogged, carbon monoxide could backup into the basement and the carbon monoxide will then be sent throughout the house. These older types of furnaces are easy to recognize because they have huge openings in the furnace casing. You can test CO_2 with an inexpensive handheld device.

The main reason a furnace needs to be replaced is because the walls in the heat exchanger break down because of age. If the walls are in bad shape, carbon monoxide could mix with the air being sent into the house.  This usually happens after 15 or 20 years. It is a potentially lethal situation. If it happens, the furnace or the heat exchanger will need to be replaced.

Warm air systems are good because the air can be kept clean and humidified, and dust particles can be kept out of the air with a filter. There will be one of three types of filters on the furnace, disposable, washable, and electronic, which is designed to take pollen and dust out of the air. Some furnaces have a humidifier that is turned on and off by a sensor that monitors the amount of humidity in the air and turns on and off accordingly.

Warm air systems are also cheaper to replace than a boiler. You do not have to worry about any pipes freezing and bursting if you do not use the heating system for a few days. It is also easy to install central air conditioning with warm air systems. The existing ducts and the blower in the furnace can be used to distribute cool air throughout the house.

The biggest drawback to warm air systems is the potential for poisonous gases to be sent throughout the entire house. Also, if the house is heated using multi-zoned system, each zone with be controlled by a motorized damper in the heating ducts. When heat is not needed in a particular zone, the damper will close to stop the warmth from going into that zone. However, the damper will not be tight enough to seal out all the air. The result is reduced efficiency. In some homes, there will be more than one furnace supplying the heat. That way when one zone does not need heat, the furnace for that zone can be idle.

GRAVITY WARM AIR

A gravity warm air system has no blower to distribute the air throughout the house. This type of system is found in some older homes. You can tell a gravity warm air system because it has several ducts sticking out of a rather large furnace. The only parts of the system are the mechanism controlling the thermostat and the burner control. The system takes advantage of the fact that warm air rises. This system makes it hard to achieve equal heat distribution. The warmer the room gets, the less the air will circulate because there will not be a great amount of cold air to be pushed around. The circulation is so weak that it can be stopped by a dirty filter in the system.

Gravity systems are tough and can last much longer than most other types of heating, but their inefficiency and lack of effectiveness make them a bad choice for heating. Their saving grace is that it is rather easy to upgrade a gravity warm air system to a forced warm air system. A blower and a motor assembly are basically all that is required.

FORCED WARM AIR

Forced warm air is the most common form of heating because it is inexpensive to install and is versatile. It is also efficient since it provides a comfortable temperature easier than with other heating systems.

Forced warm air systems are controlled by a thermostat, a fan control, and a control for the temperature of the air. When the thermostat dips to a certain temperature, it will cause the furnace to kick on and heat some air. The fan control will sense when the furnace heats up and will click the blower on, which circulates warm air through the house. The blower usually turns on when the temperature reaches between 110° and 120°F. The furnace will shut off when the temperature reaches the thermostat's setting. However, the blower will keep going until the temperature in the heat exchange dips back down to about 85°F. The fan should begin to blow warm air before the furnace clicks off. Otherwise, if the blower waits, it may pump out air that is too hot for comfort.

There are two basic ways that forced air furnaces send the warm air throughout the house. One way is the radial configuration and the other way is extended-plenum. With radial configuration, there are many different branch ducts rather than a central duct. Looking at it from above, the multiple ducts coming from the furnace resemble a spider. This type of system is usually found only in smaller homes. A similar type of system is the perimeter-loop duct, which has a duct that goes around the perimeter of the house and is connected to the furnace through feeder ducts. An extended-plenum has a large feeder duct that runs in a straight line along the length of the house and is connected to the furnace. Other ducts branch from this feeder duct and supply each room with heat. This system is good for resisting airflow and also provides adequate heat to rooms that are farthest from the furnace.

Both systems have ducts that are either rounded or rectangular. The rounded ducts are usually only about four to six inches in diameter. The rounded ducts are more resistant to airflow and are not used to supply the cool air that an air conditioner pumps out. Both systems also have return ducts made out of sheet metal. Each system will also have a separation between where the duct begins and the furnace. This separation stops the sound of the blower from being carried throughout the house.

CONDENSING FURNACES

With the cost of fuel going up, condensing furnaces are a good alternative. They are about 30 percent more efficient than conventional furnaces. With all furnaces now being required to be at least 80 percent efficient, conventional furnaces are no longer being installed in homes. Condensing furnaces are more efficient because they have a second heat exchanger. This secondary exchanger takes heat from the exhaust gases that flow up the chimney with conventional furnaces. As the temperature in the exhaust gases drops, it condenses into water vapor and releases more heat. The temperature of the gases in the flue is about 300°F to 400°F less than the flue gases in a conventional furnace's flue.

There are certain added parts in a condensing furnace so that it operates with added efficiency. The main part is an induced draft blower, also known as a power vent fan. This blower is needed to push past the added resistance caused by the secondary heat exchanger. Also, because the secondary heat exchanger makes the temperature of the gases lower, the chimney that is needed in a conventional furnace is not needed with a condensing furnace. The gases traveling through the flue are sent through plastic piping and pushed out of the house through the wall or roof. There is also a drainage pipe for the condensation, and if the furnace has a sealed combustion system that uses outside air, there is also an intake air duct.

PULSE COMBUSTION FURNACE

Pulse combustion furnaces heat by using a gas and air to create 60 to 70 small explosions per second. Pulse combustion furnaces are similar to condensing furnaces. They are efficient and they use the heat from the exhaust gases. The one difference is that the pulse combustion heats by using the small explosions of gas and air every second but the condensing furnaces heat with the constant burning of fuel.

CENTRAL HEATING WITH A HEAT PUMP

A heat pump is used to provide a house with central heating. It is pretty much the same as a forced warm air system but the way the heat is generated differs and it is used to provide cool air as well. The air is not heated by an oil or gas burner. It is heated by the air-conditioning system's being reversed. The heat pump may be large enough to provide enough cold air in the summer but will not supply enough warm air in the winter. If the heat pump is in a colder climate, the house will need some sort of other heating supply. There are other heating systems that can be hooked in with the heat pump and activated when the heat pump is no longer able to heat the house sufficiently.

HOT WATER SYSTEMS

Hot water systems are operated by a boiler. With this type of system, water is heated in the boiler and then circulated throughout the house through pipes. The hot water runs into radiators where it gives off its heat into each room. Cold water then flows back to the furnace. The pipes and the radiators are constantly filled with water. When the water is heated, it expands. To stop the expansion from bursting pipes or causing other damage, there is a holding tank to hold the expanded water until it cools down enough to return to the main water distribution system.

Boilers are made from steel or cast iron. Steel boilers are not as durable as cast iron. Steel can corrode but cast iron is resistant to corrosion. Steel boilers usually last only 15 to 20 years. Cast iron boilers have been known to last for more than 25 years.

Sometimes boilers need to be replaced because they become inefficient and too costly to operate. It will also need to be replaced when there is a leak that cannot be patched. If you can see into the firebox of the boiler, check whether water is dripping into it while the boiler is running. If the boiler has not been operated in a day or two, dripping could simply be condensation. It could also mean there is a joint that is slightly open. When the pipes heat up, they should expand and the joint should swell shut. However, if water is dripping, you should consult a professional.

In a warm climate, you may come across a water heater that is being used to supply the heat for an entire house. The small tank will only put out enough heat to keep an addition warm. Another problem is the life expectancy of hot water heaters. Most of them only last about seven years, and they are guaranteed for a much shorter life than that.

Most boilers can be modified so that they heat the water that is used in the house. When the boiler needs to heat the water for the house, the burner needs to operate all year long, not just during the colder months. Therefore, the thermostat in the house controls the circulating pump instead of the burner. The circulating pump is responsible for distributing the hot water to the radiators throughout the house when heat is needed. When there is no need for heat, a flow-control valve on the main distribution line stops the hot water from automatically rising into the distribution lines. The burner in the boiler is controlled by an aquastat that keeps track of the temperature of the water to be used by the people in the home.

The water pressure in the heating system is usually between 12 and 22 PSI. There is rarely a reason to put more water into the system, but just in case, there is a device that can automatically refill the system with water. It takes the water from the house water supply, holds it, and ensures that the PSI is reduced enough so that it can enter the boiler. There should also be a pressure release valve on the boiler. Sometimes it is located away from the boiler on the main distribution line – not a good place for it. If the boiler does not have a relief valve on it, you will need to have one installed.

All systems that use hot water should have a temperature and a pressure gauge. Older systems will have two separate gauges while the newer systems have combination gauges. The older systems have a pressure gauge and a temperature gauge that will resemble a pencil. The combination gauges will show pressure in PSI and in altitude. You do not have to worry about the altitude reading but know that it shows how high the hot water can travel to heat a room. For example, if it shows almost 28 feet (roughly equivalent to 12 PSI, it will send heat to any radiator that is about 28 feet above the boiler. The PSI should be 12 PSI. Usually if the pressure becomes greater than 30, the release valve will trigger.

The best place to have a radiator is near a window or a door on the outside wall of the home. Older homes may have freestanding cast iron radiators. Unless you like the old look, they should be replaced. Baseboard convector radiators are preferred because they distribute heat better. They are low to the ground so that heat rises and warms the room evenly. Baseboard convector radiators are also less noticeable. The final type of radiator you may come across is a freestanding convector. Any type of freestanding radiator is not efficient, and you should consider replacing it.

GRAVITY HOT WATER

This type of system follows the same principle as the warm air gravity system: hot water rises. Therefore, it will rise into the distribution pipes and force the cooler water through the pipes and back into the boiler where the water can be heated again. You should be able to recognize this type of system because the pipes are about three inches in diameter instead of the one inch in most forced systems. This type of system is no longer used because it is inefficient and often unresponsive to the demands for heat so that you will not find it in newer homes.

Gravity hot water systems come in two categories: open and closed. Open gravity systems have an overflow pipe running from the expansion tank, which must be higher than the highest radiator for that radiator to fill with water. The pipe usually runs all the way to the attic and empties to the outside through the side of the house or the roof. If the tank is located in a place with no heat, such as an attic, it must have insulation to prevent loss of heat and to protect it from freezing should the system malfunction. An open gravity system does not need a release valve. Pressure is released through the overflow pipe.

In a closed system, the expansion tank is completely closed. The tank is usually placed beside the boiler and allows for smaller radiators.

Closed system expansion tanks can also be broken down into two separate categories: diaphragm and air cushion. The diaphragm expansion tank was developed because the air cushion expansion tank is susceptible to being waterlogged because it holds trapped air in it so that there is a cushion, which is pressed as the water expands and goes into the tank. As the air escapes, it creates waterlogging. When this happens, pressure builds up quickly every time the system is turned on. The increased pressure causes the pressure relief valve to get rid of some of the water. The only way to fix the tank is to drain it and reinstall the air cushion. But with the diaphragm expansion tank, the air cushion is separated from the water by a rubberized diaphragm. Generally the diaphragm does prevent waterlogging but it can fail and allow some water-logging to occur.

FORCED HOT WATER

Boilers for forced hot water systems are not large at all when compared to the older boilers that were used for gravity systems or were once coal fired. Recognizing a forced hot water system is relatively easy. All forced hot water systems have a circulating pump inside the distribution return pipe just above the point where it runs back into the boiler. As with furnaces, there are many different types of boilers.

CONDENSING BOILERS

Condensing boilers work similarly to condensing furnaces.

They are highly efficient, and they take heat from exhaust gases that would normally flow up the flue and use it to heat water. The process actually raises the boiler's efficiency from about 60 percent to 87 percent. Cooling of the exhaust gases also eliminates the need for a chimney to vent hot gases. Gases are cooled to a point that they can be vented by way of plastic piping through a side wall. They also require an air intake duct along with a power vent, and they need to have a way to deal with the drainage from condensation.

PULSE BOILERS

Pulse boilers are even more efficient than condensing boilers. They are gas fired and operate at about 90 percent efficiency. They heat water by firing a gas and air mixture 60 to 70 times per second. They can be noisy so a vibration controller is often put between the connecting pipes and boiler to help keep the noise down. Their efficiency depends on taking the heat from the exhaust gases.

Pros/Cons

As with any type of heating system, there are advantages of having a forced hot water system. This type of system can heat a whole house including areas below the boiler. It is relatively quiet while heating and it tends to heat rooms evenly. Finally, the best advantage of forced hot water heating is that it provides zoned heating so that multiple thermostats control temperatures in the house. For example, one part of the house could be heated to 72 degrees while the rest of the house is being heated to 64 degrees, saving energy and money, a savings in colder climates. If a house does not have zone heating, any forced hot water system can be converted into one easily. The other advantages of the forced hot water system are that they are quiet while heating and they tend to heat rooms evenly.

Each heating zone can operate off its own circulating pump, or it can all operate off one pump. If there is only one circulating pump, each zone is controlled by a valve operated by the thermostat. When one thermostat calls for heat, the circulating pump will begin delivering heat to that one zone through just the one zone valve that needs it and so on with other zones. If there is a circulating pump for each zone, the thermostat will call for heat to a zone, and the burner and circulating pump will begin working. As long as the burner is already working, any other zone that needs heat will simply start its own circulating pump so that hot water will be pumped into the zones' heating elements.

Of course, all heating systems have drawbacks. Because forced hot water systems heat with water, the water in the pipes could freeze, and the pipes could burst. This could happen if power is lost for an extended period of time or if the boiler stops working during a particularly cold spell. When you are inspecting the home, look for pipes that may run too close to outside windows. These sections of the pipes should be insulated as they will be the first sections to freeze.

DISTRIBUTION PIPING

There are three basic types of distribution piping: one-pipe, two-pipe, and series loop. The system that is used depends on the size of the house.

The one-pipe system has one pipe that leaves the boiler and travels throughout the house and then back to the boiler. It serves as both the supply pipe and the return pipe. Each radiator in the house is connected to two risers at each end that are connected to the one-pipe system. A shutoff valve on the riser allows water to flow into the radiator. This way a radiator can be shut off without affecting other radiators farther down the line. The farther the radiators are from the boiler, the cooler the water that reaches them. As a result, these radiators have to be larger so that they produce the same amount of heat.

The two-pipe system is the most costly to install. As the name suggests, there are two pipes that are used for this system. One pipe is used to supply the heated water and the other is used to return the water to the boiler. This allows even heating throughout homes because the cool water going back to the boiler never mixes with the hot water going to the boiler. While it is relatively costly to install this system, it is often worth it because of the quality of the heat it provides.

The series loop system is the least expensive and easiest system to install. Heated water flows from the boiler and throughout the house in one pipe. It enters each radiator, usually a baseboard convector, goes through radiators one by one. Therefore, if the supply is stopped at one radiator, it cannot continue on to any of the other radiators. This type of system is used in smaller homes. In a larger home, the system is usually divided into multiple heating zones so that each zone will have a different set of supply pipes. Each zone will also either have its own circulating pump or its own valve that is controlled by a thermostat in the main supply pipe.

The supply pipes do not always run to a radiator. A forced hot water system could also supply heat through distribution piping imbedded in the floor, walls, or ceilings. These areas are known as heating panels and they serve the same purpose as radiators. The heat from the pipes is transferred to the panels and the panels heat the room through radiation and convection. This type of system heats rooms evenly and is most effective when the house has no basement.

STEAM HEATING SYSTEMS

Boilers used for steam heat are similar to boilers used for hot water systems. They are made of cast iron or steel, but there is a difference in the gauges and controls. The main difference is that there is a water level gauge on a boiler that is used for steam heat. This gauge is not present on a boiler for a hot water heating systems. Steam heat is seldom installed anymore. They work by boiling water in the boiler and then distributing the steam. The boiler is only filled about 75 percent with water, which is heated to the boiling point. Then steam rises through pipes to radiators after passing through air vents. The steam is hot and when it contacts the cool radiator, it gives off heat causing the stream to turn back into water. The water then flows back to the boiler for reheating. If the air vent is blocked, pressure will build up and not allow steam to enter the radiator, stopping heat from entering the room. The faulty air filter should be replaced.

All steam heating systems should have a thermostat along with a high pressure limit switch, a valve that would automatically relieve pressure, and a low water cutoff. There should also be two gauges: a water-level gauge and a pressure gauge.

An electrical connection between the high pressure limit switch and the burner control stops high pressure from building by shutting down the burner. The high pressure limit switch should be connected directly to the boiler by a pipe that looks like a pig tail. There is water in the bottom of the pig tail that prevents the control from corroding.

The pressure relief valve is set up to relieve pressure from the system if the pressure becomes greater than it is designed to be. Most systems operate at about two PSI. However, a relief valve on a residential system will usually be set to relieve pressure at 15 PSI.

A low-water cutoff will stop the burner in a boiler when the water level drops to an unacceptable level. The cutoff can be inside or outside the boiler, but outside is better so that it is easy to test if the system is working correctly. If the control is outside, the unit will have a blow off valve that needs to be cleaned periodically. The maker of the valves recommends flushing the valve once a month by opening the valve and blowing it down. Failure to flush the valve results in sludge build-up, preventing the valve from working properly. Make sure you open the valve. If nothing comes out or if something thick oozes out, you know it has not been flushed in recent history. If the valve is inside the boiler, it is self-cleaning and requires no flushing.

The boiler has a water level gauge that will allow you to see how much water is in the boiler. It may be covered with sediment make it impossible to read. If this is the case, it should be cleaned so that it can be read. The gauge is usually located on the side of the boiler. In fact, if the low water cutoff is outside the boiler, the water level gauge will probably be part of the assembly. The exact position of the water gauge is not important but it should be somewhere between one half and two thirds full. If you cannot see the water level at all, there is a problem. If the boiler is completely filled with water, the system could well be flooded. The water will then fill the boiler, the distribution pipes, and the radiators. Most of the time the fittings and the valves on the radiators are not watertight. If this is the case, water will run out of the radiator and flood the room. If there is not enough water in the system or if the gauge shows it is completely empty, more water must be run into the boiler. The line supplying the water can be opened manually. Sometimes the system will have an automatic water feeder that will refill the system as needed. However, these systems have been known to malfunction for a variety of reasons.

DISTRIBUTION PIPING

There are two types of distribution piping for steam heating systems: one-pipe and two-pipe. If only one pipe is connected to the radiator, it is a one-pipe distribution system. If two pipes are connected to the radiator, it is a two-pipe distribution system.

Just as the name suggests, the one-pipe distribution system has one pipe to deliver the steam and provide a means for the condensation to return to the boiler. The radiators have to be pitched so that condensation flows back out of the radiator instead of building up and blocking the delivery of steam. Each radiator is equipped with an air vent and a manually adjustable supply valve. Some air vents can be adjusted manually as well. These vents can be opened or closed to allow more or less air out of the radiator. Opening and closing the air vents allow the entire house to be heated equally and works well in larger homes. Radiators closer to the boiler have more heat and are able to heat their rooms sooner than the radiators farther from the boiler. By controlling the air vents, a radiator can be adjusted to allow less air to escape into one room so that rooms needing more heat receive more warm air. The air vent in the heated room would be decreased while the air vent in the room where more heat is needed would be increased.

A two-pipe distribution system uses one pipe to provide the steam to the radiators and another one to return condensation back to the boiler for heating. There is no air vent on these radiators. Heat is controlled by a steam trap that allows air and condensation to run through the pipes, but it stops the steam from reaching the radiator. Unlike a one-pipe steam system, a two-pipe steam system can be converted into a forced hot water system.

For both the one- and the two-pipe systems if the condensation return line is below the boiler, it is considered a wet return. If the return line is above the boiler, it is considered a dry return. For a wet return, a Hartford loop should be present. It is a special arrangement of pipes that helps prevent water from leaking from the boiler when the wet-return piping springs a leak. In case of a leak in the return piping, water will continue to drain down until it reaches the Hartford loop where it will be stopped and prevent any damage to the boiler if it continues to fire. If you do not see a Hartford loop during your inspection, you should consider having one installed.

Pros/Cons

There are two major drawbacks to using a steam heating system. The first is the fact that it is slow to react when there is a sudden need for heat production. Steam heat only works once the water is boiled and then the steam is distributed throughout the home. Also, unless the pipes that return the condensation to the boiler have a pump, the boiler must be located below the lowest radiators.

The major advantages of the steam heating systems are more noticeable in larger buildings. There is no need for a fan or pump to help circulate steam. Water does not remain in the pipes so that there is no threat of the pipes freezing and bursting, and there is no need to drain water during repairs. Also, if a leak occurs, little water leaks out.

OIL BURNERS

Most homes in the United States have heating systems that are fueled by oil or gas. Most coal burners were upgraded to oil burners in the late 1940s. Oil is stored in a tank that can be below or above ground. A filter and a shutoff valve are located at the tank or at the oil pump. If the oil tank is above ground, you will be able to inspect it. If it is below ground, there is no way to check the tank without digging.

The first thing you should check is the overall condition of the oil tank. Make sure the tank is solid and in decent shape. It should not have rusted legs or legs that are digging into the ground or buckling under the weight of the tank. Make sure there are a shutoff valve and a filter between the tank and the oil pump. You may also want to check if there is fuel in the tank. You can do this by tapping on the bottom of the tank. If it sounds hollow, the tank is probably empty. If the system is not working when you check it, it may be because there is no fuel in the tank.

Your inspection should also include the simple test of look, smell, and listen. As was explained earlier in this chapter, be sure to perform a thorough visual check of the heating system. Make sure you cannot smell fuel oil in the basement. When the system is operating, make sure you do not hear any strange noises.

Operation of the oil burner is complicated. First, the oil goes into an oil pump. The circulator motor is located at the bottom and the center of the oil burning system. The oil pump is located on the left of the circulator motor. Oil is pressurized by the pump and sent through a nozzle into a combustion chamber. The oil is then ignited and burns with the help of air supplied by a blower operated by the same motor as the oil pump.

There are a few checks that you should do for an oil burner. The first thing you should do is look into the inspection hole checking for oil that has pooled inside. If you find oil, do not start up the system. If there is no pooling oil, fire up the system and look, listen, and smell. Make sure the barometric damper, located in the exhaust flue, swings open and then closed again. If it does not open or stays closed, it needs to be readjusted. If the system does not fire up at all and you know there is oil and the breaker is on, try resetting the system. There is one reset button in the control box and another at the flue. Press each button once but not more than once. If the button continues to trip, there must be a reason for it. Consult a professional or inform the owners that they need to have the system checked out.

ELECTRIC HEATING

There are several different types of electrical heating systems: electric forced air furnaces, electric water furnaces, and electric baseboards. Furnaces powered by electricity are easy and quick to install. Basically just one cable and one wire need to run from a power source to a furnace, and the system is ready to go. The major disadvantage is that the unit will heat the entire house when only one room needs to be heated.

Electric forced air furnaces can be any size. They distribute heat through ducts, or they push air directly into the room. Forced air systems pull in cool air through a grill or a duct that extends to a distant place. The air is heated by being pulled through elements that are hot, and a blower distributes the heated air.

The forced air electric furnace should be inspected as any other warm air system needs to be inspected. Electric furnaces are unique because the flow of electricity is staggered so it takes some time it to create sufficient heat.

An electric water furnace is a boiler that runs on electricity instead of oil or gas. Unlike boilers, electric water heaters are small and are usually placed on a wall. A heater is usually just a box that has a cold water pipe running into it and a hot water pipe running away from it. Water is pushed out of the heater and into the distribution line by a circulator. When you inspect this type of furnace, run the system and make sure the outgoing line is hot. If it is, the system is working.

Electric baseboard heating is quick and easy to install. It is also durable and rarely breaks down. However, if it does, that is only one individual heater that is broken. All the other baseboard electric heaters will continue to work because each unit operates individually. Most baseboard heaters are 240 volts, meaning they must have two hot input feeders that need to run into the heating element to produce heat. Each heater is controlled by a thermostat that is usually on the heater itself but can be on the wall beside the heater. The thermostat will be either a single pole or a double pole thermostat, and you can tell the difference by checking if the thermostat has an off switch on it.

A single pole thermostat has one wire running to the heater and a second wire being controlled by the thermostat. It is not possible for the thermostat to be turned completely off. The only way to turn the baseboard heater off is to throw the circuit breaker that controls it. If you notice a single pole thermostat while performing an inspection, make a note of it because the heater will not be able to be on in some rooms and off in others.

A double-pole thermostat controls two wires, allowing the thermostat to be turned off completely. The circuit breaker does not have to be tripped to turn off the baseboard heater, making it more convenient if the room is not used often.

A thermostat mounted on the wall will be a single- or a double-pole thermostat. However, single pole thermostats are not allowed to be installed anymore. This means you should not see too many of the single pole thermostats. Again, you will be able to tell whether the thermostat is single or double by checking to see if there is an off switch on the thermostat.

To test the baseboard heater, all you need to do is turn the thermostat up. The baseboard heater will make a fast ticking noise as the heating elements heat up. You may also smell dust and any other debris burning off the elements. If the baseboard heater does not turn on, check to make sure the breaker is not off.

You also need to check the location of the electrical outlets around the baseboard heaters. The receptacles should not be above the heater. If they are, the power cord could loop down and get caught in the heating element of the heater. Or the cord could hang too close to the heater, become dry and crack. As the insulation breaks and falls away, the hot conductors will be exposed. The correct place for the outlets is between and/or below two heaters or, better yet, to have them integrated into the system. Many baseboard heaters are sold with an end that allows an electrical outlet to be mounted right in the frame assembly. Finally, make sure the heater is not directly wired to the receptacle. Turn off the power to the heater and then test the electrical outlet with a plug-in tester. If it does not have power, the heater is not wired correctly and needs to be rewired.

WOOD STOVES

Wood burning stoves are not the primary source of heat for most homes. They are usually used to heat one or two rooms.

Sometimes they have been installed by the previous homeowner to help defray some energy costs. Regardless, you need to inspect a wood stove thoroughly. Wood stoves that are improperly installed are a major cause of home fires.

You want to make sure that the area directly around the stove is some type of masonry, rocks, or stone. There should be a short piece of the flue above the stove that runs parallel to the stove. Make sure there is proper space between the stove and anything else that is flammable. Each area has its own laws regarding how wood burning stoves should be installed. If possible, you will want to consult the manufacturer's installation requirements or the National Fire Protection Association (NFPA) at **www.nfpa.org**. When checking clearances, remember that some stoves do not need as much clearance because they have built in heat shields. For example, jacketed stoves can be closer to combustible materials, but check the manufacturer's instructions to determine how much clearance is needed.

The normal clearance between the stove and combustible materials is at least three feet. Make sure there are no flammable materials in the three-foot clearance zone. Flammable materials to watch for are rugs, curtains, studs, and furniture. Non-flammable materials, such as bricks, may be used to shield a flammable wall from the stove's heat. This material needs to be one inch out from the wall so that air can circulate between the protective material and the wall.

Again, there are regulations to follow depending on the type and the geographic location of the stove. If a nonflammable shield is used, clearance above the stove can be reduced to one foot, but the shield should be placed at least one inch away from the flammable surface. Also, the shield needs to be at least 22-gauge and it must continue along the flammable surface until the surface is at least three feet from the stove.

A nonflammable floor should be under the stove, but certain stoves can be placed on a combustible material if they have the proper legs or pedestals and if hollow masonry is also installed. The stove could also be placed in a layer of brick, stone, or a similar substance. In this case the stove needs to stand at least six inches off the floor and the brick (or other nonflammable material) must be at least two inches thick. The nonflammable flooring must extend for at least 18 inches on all sides of a wood-burning stove.

You need to look closely at the flue pipe extending from the stove to the chimney. The flue pipe should be as short as possible.

Its slope should slightly increase and it should never slope downward before it enters the chimney. Make sure it is sealed where it enters the chimney. There should be no gaps in the piping. All sections of the pipe should not be just fitted together; they need to be screwed together. Also, to determine how much clearance is needed between the flue pipe and flammable materials, take the diameter of the flue pipe and multiply it by three. That is the necessary clearance. There should be at least two inches from the point that the flue meets the chimney and flammable materials. Local codes may require more clearance. Ask if the chimney has been inspected recently. There are many things that could go wrong inside and outside the chimney so have it checked by a professional.

All stoves have a damper in the stove pipe. It is a plate that pivots inside the pipe and controls air entering the pipe. The damper can be opened and closed by a rod that runs through it and out the side of the stove pipe. By opening and closing the damper, you control the amount of combustion inside the stove. If the fire gets out of control or if a flue fire ignites, the air to the flue can be completely closed off with the flue.

You may find a catalytic converter with the wood stove, which helps the stove generate more heat. They need to be clean of ashes and other debris. Most will last only five or six years so that you should see if there is a tag listing the year it was made. If not, make a note that the converter may need to be cleaned or replaced soon.

FIREPLACES

Fireplaces are not a great source of heat but they are a nice feature to any home. They can be inspected easily. There are two

 types: metal inserts and masonry. Metal inserts are prefabricated and they have masonry all around them. Masonry fireplaces are the more traditional looking fireplaces with brick or possibly rock and mortar.

Look at the fireplace from a few feet away to see if the masonry has any major cracks. Do not worry about tiny cracks. Use a powerful flashlight, a pair of goggles, and a pair of gloves to look up into the chimney. Make sure the damper works properly. Try to look up into the flue to make sure it has a liner to help all the smoke and gases exit the house safely. If the lining is broken, harmful gases could escape into the house and cause illness or even death. A broken lining could also lead to a fire. It may be difficult to see under the creosote build-up to verify that the lining is in good shape. Generally, houses built after 1950 have liners. If you do not see the liner extending up and out of the chimney there may not be one. The lining is important to the overall welfare of the fireplace and the entire home that you may want to have a professional inspect the unit.

Although it is difficult to inspect the inside of the chimney, it is relatively easy to inspect the outside. Is it solid and completely together or is it falling apart? Are there creosote stains leaking out between the joints? If so, the flue liner may be broken. If you can see parts of the flue liner and it is metal, make sure it is not discolored or warped. It is possible that there was a flue fire that could cause the flue liner to collapse or crack. It could also cause the mortar to fall apart and the tiles to crack. Other signs of a previous flue fire include bubbly and colorful creosote, a bulging rain cap, and smoke stains around cracks in the mortar joints.

Just as various jurisdictions have different requirements for a stove or fireplace, they may also have different requirements about the outside of a chimney. Be sure to know what is required on the house you are inspecting. Some extras it may require are a wash cap, a spark arrester, or a flat metal cap on unused chimneys.

More houses are being built with gas fireplaces, which are much safer than wood-burning fireplaces. There are two types of gas fireplaces: vented and unvented. Vented fireplaces have gases venting to the outside. Unvented fireplaces do not and could prove to be a problem because gases are being vented into the home. As long as the unvented fireplaces are working correctly, there is no problem. These types of fireplaces are supposed to shut down if a problem occurs, but that does not always happen. Therefore, if the unvented fireplace begins to malfunction, it could cause tiredness, sickness, or even death from carbon monoxide poisoning.

COOLING

Depending on the climate, you may run across many homes that have central air or air conditioning. Central air cools down homes by taking the air in the house and cooling it while also removing the extra moisture. Air is pulled in across a cooling coil removing some of the moisture in the cool air, which is then distributed through the house.

An air conditioner has four basic parts: a compressor, a condenser, an expansion device, and an evaporator. The first three parts work together to help the cooling coil (also known as the evaporator) do its job. Air conditioners use a refrigerant, usually a gas at normal atmospheric pressure and temperature. However, as the cooling system applies pressure to the refrigerant and removes the absorbed heat, the gas turns into a liquid. Then the pressure is released and the refrigerant changes back to a gas. This change causes the gas to take in the heat that is surrounding it, which causes the air passing over the evaporator to cool.

A central air conditioning system is closed and should never need refrigerant added to it. However, refrigerant may begin to leak out when small cracks develop in the lines and pipes begin to loosen. Additional refrigerant may be added and can continue to be added so that the system will continue to work. However, if so much refrigerant begins to leak out that it needs to be added more than once per season, the system will need to be checked and the leaks will have to be repaired.

Air conditioners are rated in either British thermal units (BTUs) or tons. Basically one ton equals 12,000 BTUs. To find out if the air conditioning system is large enough for the house, figure that for every 550 square feet there needs to be 12,000 BTUs or one ton. Therefore, if the house has 2,200 square feet, it requires an air conditioner with 48,000 BTUs or four tons.

The air conditioner should either be just the right size for the house or a little too small. It should never be too large. If it is too large, it will cool the house down quickly and then shut off.

While it is off, the evaporator will become cool and be unable to remove enough moisture from air in the house, making the air humid and uncomfortable. Therefore, the compressor on an air conditioning unit will run all the time. If the system is really too small, it will not cool the home.

INTEGRAL COOLING SYSTEM

The integral cooling system is one of two types. This type of system is less expensive than the split type, but it is also noisier. The integral system is sometimes known as a single package unit. As this name suggests, all the components of the air conditioner are contained in one housing. These units are usually installed in an attic or a crawl space. They usually have ducts extending to the outside of the house so that air can be pulled in to go across the evaporator.

SPLIT COOLING SYSTEM

Split cooling systems have components split into separate locations—the compressor and condenser are located outside the house, allowing the system to pull in outside air. They also run quieter. The evaporator and the expansion device are inside the home. Their location depends on the type of heating in the house. If the house has a forced warm system, the  evaporator will be located with the furnace where it can use the furnace blower to distribute the air to the house. If the home has another type of heating system, the evaporator will be located in the attic and have its own blower. If there is no attic, the evaporator can be in the basement or a closet. The split unit is connected by two pipes that allow the refrigerant to go back and forth. These pipes are made of copper, and one will be much larger than the other. The smaller pipe carries the liquid refrigerant from the condenser to the expansion device. The larger line carries the refrigerant from the evaporator to the compressor. The larger pipe, known as the suction line, should be insulated.

YOUR INSPECTION

Exactly how much you can inspect the system will depend on the air temperature outside. If it is cooler than 60°F outside, you should not turn on the air conditioning unit because operating it at cooler temperatures could harm the compressor. If you cannot run the system, you should get a guarantee from the owner that the system works properly.

If the temperature is above 60°F, you will be able to run the system and check it out. While you are standing next to the compressor, have someone turn down the thermostat so the compressor will kick on. The compressor is the most expensive part of the system to replace. Unfortunately, it is also the most important. Compressors usually last about 10 years. Its life is directly linked to the local climate. If the climate is warm, the compressor probably will not last 10 years but if it is somewhere cooler than it may last 15 years. Listen to the compressor and make sure there are no unusual noises. It should start up smoothly and run continuously, making a low humming noise. If there are grunting, straining, or high-pitched squealing noises, or if the unit starts and stops repeatedly, it needs to be checked by a professional.

The fan on the unit should start up at the same time as the compressor. Either look into the unit to see if the fan is spinning or place your hand over the unit and feel for a rush of air. After about 15 or 20 minutes, the fan should expel warm air from the heat created when the refrigerant was compressed. If the air does not turn warm, there is probably something wrong with the compressor. It will need to be checked out by a professional.

After the system has been operational, the compressor listened to, and the fan checked, go to the suction line. It should be covered with insulation. Find a gap in the insulation. The pipe should be cool to the touch. There may be condensation on the line, which is fine, but there should be no frost on the line, which would mean the refrigerant is deficient, and while the system will still work, it will not be efficient. Sometimes you will find a little window on the line, known as a sight glass used to let the homeowner know there is a problem with the line. The refrigerant is clear so that if you do not see anything through the glass, things are fine, but if you see bubbles passing by the window, the refrigerant is low. Make a note of it.

This would also be a good time to check the registers. Make sure there is cool air coming out of them at a decent rate. If the air does not seem cool enough or powerful enough, there is a problem with the system. It could be any number of things, but you should know that it is not working correctly.

The location of the compressor and condenser is important. They should be away from a great deal of sunlight so that they can cool the air more easily. They should also be free of shrubbery and other obstructions. There should be at least one foot between the unit and anything else; otherwise proper air flow will not occur. This unit can be noisy so that it should be placed on a concrete slab or pre-cast concrete blocks so that there will be no vibration. Also, the unit should be level so that no settling will happen.

You should also notice that there is a disconnect switch located somewhere near the compressor. This switch will allow a maintenance person to work on the system without being worried that someone inside the house will turn down the thermostat while the system is being worked on. Finally, check the overall condition of the unit to make sure it is clean and free of debris.

You may find a water-cooled air conditioner instead of air cooled like the units we have been discussing. Usually water-cooled systems are only used in larger apartment buildings because they are much too costly to operate in homes. They would require far too much water to allow the system to cool a home. If you come across a system that is water cooled, it should probably be replaced with a less expensive system.

The next thing to check is the evaporator. If it is located in the attic, it will probably have refrigerant lines snaking up the outside wall and into the house to the attic. If it is located in the basement, the lines will not be long and they will run right into the structure. If you can, look at the evaporator. As with the lines, dripping water is fine but frosting is not okay because it indicates that something is wrong with the flow of air in the system.

If the evaporator is located in the furnace plenum, you will see the refrigerant lines running into the sheet metal that covers the plenum. Under the evaporator coil you should see a pan that collects water from condensation on the coil. A drain line runs from the plenum to carry water away from the evaporator. You should see a U-shaped trap where the drain line and the plenum meet, allowing water to pass through. If it is missing, it needs to be replaced.

Usually condensed water will run through a plastic drain line and be taken out of the house in one of four ways. The drain may run to a sink where the water drips down the drain. It may run to the outside and drip down on the outer side of the foundation, or it may run to and drip down a small hole in the basement slab. If it runs through the foundation there should be a splash plate so that the dripping water is directed away from the wall. A drain line that runs to a hole in the slab is not the best way to get rid of the water. If the water table is high or the dirt has a high concentration of clay, water could slowly build up and create problems with seepage. Occasionally water will run into a pump positioned near the furnace. The pump is rectangular and is used to pump water out high enough so that it can flow away from the system in any number of ways. The pump is activated when water reaches a certain level. To check it, pour water into its reservoir until it kicks on. If it does not work, it will need to be fixed or replaced.

Check around the evaporator and the entire furnace to see if there is any sign of past water leakage that could result in the heat exchanger's being damaged. If you see mineral and rust deposits, you will probably want to get a professional to make sure the heat exchanger is not rusting or deteriorating. With the furnace turned off by the master switch, you should also check the tension of the belt that controls the blower. It controls the circulation of both the warm and cold air. (It is usually desirable to have more then one blower speed for heat and air conditioning because cold air is heavier and requires the blower to work harder.) Press the belt between the two pulleys and make sure there is not too much slack. If the belt moves in an inch or more, it needs to be adjusted.

If the evaporator is in a separate location from the furnace, it will have its own blower to distribute air through the house. Make sure that the system is mounted on cork, rubber, or Styrofoam to minimize vibrations. If it is in the attic, it can be hung from the rafters to reduce vibration.

Again, the built-up condensation will have to be removed through a drain line running through a wall, the roof, and into the gutter, or running into the plumbing vent stack. Sometimes drains are not allowed to run into the plumbing vent stack. Therefore, if you see this happening, check local plumbing codes.

If the evaporator is in the attic, check whether the ceiling below is not damaged by condensation. Sometimes the drain for condensation becomes clogged and begins to leak so that there should be an extra drain pan or another drain to remove the water in case a blockage occurs.

CONCLUSION

A heating and cooling system is complicated and can be costly to repair or replace. Even if a house seems perfect if there is a faulty heating and/or cooling system, you (or the potential buyer) will want to think twice before buying the house.

A heat pump takes the air and warms it or cools it before distributing it to the house. Heat pumps do not burn fuel. They usually are effective only in mild climates. The pump may have electric furnace coils in case the weather gets cold. The heat pump may be inside with a forced air system or it could be outside. Outside units are the least desirable because they are susceptible to extreme temperatures.

To check the system, make sure the outdoor unit is not covered with frost. Remove the outside grill and make sure the blower is not covered with frost. You will see a copper pipe running from the system into the house. While the system is running, check the pipes outside and inside to make sure one is hot and one is cold. Remember, if it is in the cooling mode, condensation is normal. Check that the drain is working and is not clogged. Finally, check the coils inside to make sure they are not frosted over.

Geothermal heating is sometimes called a water-to-air heat pump or a ground source system. This type of heating and cooling uses the temperature in the earth to transfer heat or cold to the house. Consult the owner for a verification that the system is working correctly and whether it is open or closed. An open system uses fresh water to run the system with the water usually coming from a pond or a nearby river. It is then dumped somewhere else. A closed system continues to circulate the same water over and over. You can easily check whether the system is working properly by turning the thermostat up or down until it turns on.

House Inspection Tip #8

Turn on the air conditioner to make sure that it works. Is the drainage causing any stains or damage? Make sure you look closely because replacing an air conditioning unit can be expensive.

10

APPLIANCES / UTILITY ROOM

Appliances fall into two basic categories: fixed appliances (hot water heaters and water conditioners) and movable appliances (clothes washers and dryers). Obviously, the home you inspect may not have a washer or dryer, but the house will have a hot water heater and may have a water conditioner.

Do not forget to see the appendices and the companion CD-ROM for sample checklists and forms you can use to keep track of all your findings when inspecting a home.

FIXED APPLIANCES

The first thing you should check when entering the basement is whether the bottom of the appliances show any sign of past water problems. Are they discolored or rusted at the bottom? Most of the time it is best to have appliances set on bricks, cement blocks, or treated wood.

Water Heaters

Check the size of the water heater. If it is electric, it will need to be 50 gallons and 4,500 watts to warm water for a family of four. If it is gas powered, it will need to be 40 gallons with 32,000 BTUs.

You need to check the water lines feeding into the water heater for leaks. Make sure there are no male plastic fittings screwed into female threads on the heater. Always check the temperature setting by running hot water from the faucet closest to the heater. Check the temperature with a thermometer that has a range between 100° and 200°F. If the temperature is greater than 120°F, the thermostat should be adjusted. If the water heater is covered by a jacket, make a note of it and plan to remove it. Most manufacturers void their warranty if the water heater has a jacket.

All water heaters must have a pressure and temperature relief valve to ensure that pressure does not build-up inside it. Theoretically, if too much pressure builds in the water heater, it could explode. Therefore, make sure you thoroughly inspect the valve, which should be located on the body of the water heater. However, older water heaters may have the valve located on a water line. In this case it should be installed on the hot water line just after the heater tank. If it is installed on the cold water line you should think about having the valve installed on the body. If the valve is dripping, it may be faulty. It should also have a pipe extending from it down to about three or four inches from the floor to ensure that should the valve go off, it does not spray hot water all over the tank or someone standing nearby. You should NOT open the valve and check to see if it works because it may remain open and cause other problems.

You should also check the water heater to see if there is a pan under it to catch any leaking water. If the hot water heater is located in the attic or on a floor that should not be leaked on, a pan is a necessity. Sometimes pans need to be installed as code. Otherwise, a pan may not be needed. Usually it is a good idea to have a pan installed just in case. If there are metal water pipes, there should be a bonding jumper running just above the heater from the hot water line to the cold water line to protect the installer from possible electrocution.

It is a little easier to check an electric water heater than a gas powered one. The first thing you should check on an electric water heater is that it is properly grounded. Older homes that have not been rewired will almost certainly have a water heater that is not grounded. Check that the correct size wiring is used. Most units use between 18 and 23 amps. For this amount of wattage, a heater should have 10-gauge wire. You can tell if it is 10-gauge because the jacket on the wire will read "10-2 w/g." If you do not know the wattage of the heater, it should be printed on a factory sticker located on the heater's side.

Gas powered water heaters are a little trickier to inspect. They should always be located in an area with plenty of space rather than in closets or under stairways. If there are any flammables around, the gas water heater needs to be at least 18 inches off the floor.

Check the access plate on a gas hot water heater. Make sure no flammables are near the heater, especially not directly in front of the access plate. If the access hole is not covered, flames could leap out of the heater.

Gas leaks around the fittings on hot water heaters are common.

The best way to check for leaks is to use a gas sniffer, a wand that will sound if it detects gas. Wave the wand near the fittings. If you do not have a wand, apply soapy water to all the fittings. If any bubbling occurs, you know you have a gas leak.

You should also listen to the burning of the flame inside the heater. If it makes a sound, stops, and burns quietly and then makes another sound, there is something dangerously wrong. There is either too little secondary air getting to the flame, or there is rust and debris getting into the air. You may smell gas, or your eyes may bother you. Other times a toxic gas such as carbon monoxide may be produced. If ventilation is inadequate or if the heater is in a small area, toxins can kill the occupants of the house without their ever knowing a thing. The problem of secondary air can be solved by installing louvered doors instead of solid doors. You could even cut two holes into the solid door. The holes should be spaced according to the instructions for the heater.

Just as you have to do with all types of heaters, the flue pipe for the water heater needs to be inspected. Make sure all the fittings are connected and that the pipe itself is in good shape. If the flue is a single wall pipe, it must be kept at least six inches from any flammable materials including joists and studs. Double wall pipe should be kept at least one inch from any flammables. Double wall is always a better choice to use because it does not sweat. Single wall will sweat on the inside, and the sweat will drip back down into the heater and rust it out.

The flue pipe needs to extend all the way out of the house through the roof, slanting upward. It should be connected to the heater with a hood, and there should be a rain cap on the top of the flue.

A variety of pipes can be used for gas. Recently, more flexible piping has been installed in homes. Sometimes a code prohibits the use of copper pipes for gas. Copper pipes are fine as long as the gas has sulfur removed from it. It is rare to find gas that has not had the sulfur removed from it. Be careful when dealing with flexible piping because it is leaks easily. Never try to move an appliance that is hooked into a gas line.

All gas water heaters must have a valve to stop the flow of gas from reaching the heater. Flex connectors are usually required for heaters in areas susceptible to earthquakes. There may also be a requirement to have a chain around the gas hot water heater. Any automatic gas appliance requires a dirt leg that runs between the gas line and the hot water heater. They look like an upside down "L." Gas enters from the gas pipe and must make a right angle turn to enter the heater. Any debris in the line will drop down to the bottom of the dirt leg rather than enter the heater. Make sure a dirt leg is present and that it is installed right side up; that is, the "L" needs to be upside down.

Water Conditioners

If a house has a water conditioner, simply make a note of it. If you are not familiar with them, have a professional look at it. They are installed where the main water line runs into the home. The only part of the water conditioner that you should check is the drainage line. Most water conditioners send their backwash into the house's draining system. The drain should not be directly placed into the system. There needs to be at least one inch of space so that the backwash does not enter the main water line and contaminate the house's water supply.

MOVABLE APPLIANCES

Clothes Dryers

If the previous owners leave the dryer behind, there are four points you will want to inspect if the dryer is electric: the hose connection, the vent pipe, the vent exit, and the wiring. If it is a gas dryer you will also want to check for gas leaks. You may use a sniffer or soap and water. Never move the dryer even if the gas pipes are not easily accessible.

It is quick and easy to check the dryer's appliance hose connection. Simply look behind the dryer and make sure the hose is securely fastened. If you notice lint all over the floor and/or wall then the connection is probably loose.

Local codes usually require vent pipes to be made of metal. They can be flexible or solid. Gas dryers must have metal piping. Lint can get caught in electric dryers with plastic piping—a potential fire hazard. To be safe, use metal piping for the dryer vent. You should also make sure the piping is not too long. It should not wrap around or fold over itself, making it difficult for exhaust to exit. Make sure the vent pipe is in good shape and that it is hooked-up to the vent exit. The vent pipe should never be connected to the vent exit using flammable materials.

The vent is where dryer exhaust exits the house. If the dryer vent stops inside the house, it will cause moisture to stay in the house. You also do not want the vent to terminate in a water bucket. Some homeowners outsmart themselves by trying this little trick. It does keep the heat from the dryer in the home, which may save a few dollars on the annual heating bill, but the extra moisture will rot the wood in the house and cause appliances to break. Make sure you can follow the vent and that it terminates outside the home. On the outside, the vent should have a hood on it with a flapper plate. Make sure the hood is securely fastened and that the flapper is working properly.

All dryers run on 120 and 240 volts at the same time. They should be wired with 10-gauge wiring. Most types of wiring are grandfathered in, but to be up to current code the wiring should read "10-3 NMB w/g." There should be three insulated wires and a ground wire running to the dryer. It is no longer permissible to use SEC cable.

Clothes Washers

If the washer is staying with the house, you need to check that the outlet is grounded. There is no exception to this rule. If the house is older, it is likely that the outlet is not grounded — be sure to check it. It is usually a good idea to run a washer through all its cycles to make sure it works correctly. Make sure the flexible water hose is securely connected inside the vertical washer drain pipe. Otherwise, you may flood the floor.

Check water lines that are used for the washer. The usual black hoses are not really for permanent use as water lines. These types of hoses should be turned on and off just like a regular garden hose would be. Failure to do this could cause the hose to blister and explode. To avoid having to do this, the hoses should be made to be water lines. These hoses have stainless steel braids running around them.

Even if the washer is not staying, its drain pipe needs to be inspected. It should be at least two inches in diameter and between 18 and 30 inches tall. The drain trap should be located on the same floor as the washer. It may be one floor below the washer, but it should never be on the floor above. If the washer pipe goes into the basement floor, a trap should be present. Drop a tiny pebble into the drain. If you hear a splash, you know the trap is there. If the drain empties into a laundry tub, it is okay but the tub should be secured to a wall or the floor if it is lightweight. Finally, if the washer simply drains into the backyard, it does not need a trap but you may want there to be one anyway.

CONCLUSION

It is more important to check the fixed appliances because they cost more to fix or replace. Make sure you check the water heater thoroughly. If the washer and dryer are staying with the house, check them over just to give yourself piece of mind if you are planning to buy the house. If you are inspecting the house for someone else, you may or may not be required to check the washer and dryer.

11

EXTERIOR DOOR & WINDOWS

DOORS

The front door is most visible so you should pay particular attention to its condition. It may be steel, solid-wood, or fiberglass.

Steel Doors

Steel doors have a core of foam inside them. They are commonly called steel-insulated doors. They usually come from the factory with a grey primer coat, and they are sometimes installed without any additional coating. Unpainted doors will rust. In colder climates, look for rusting at the bottom of the door from salt thrown on the doorstep to melt ice. Doors in coastal climates are also susceptible to rust.

Steel-insulated doors are inexpensive and energy efficient. Be sure to check magnetic weather strips while you are inspecting the doors. Some door frames have cheap plastic housing for the magnets so that they tear away from the frame and stick to the door, or else a pet tears away the magnetic strip.

Solid-Wood Doors

Many people choose solid wood doors because they are attractive, but they have a tendency to warp almost as soon as they are

installed. Check for signs of warping rotting, splitting, cracking, or delaminating. Also, be aware that solid-wood doors sometimes are not good at keeping the cold outside and the heat inside.

Fiberglass Doors

As with the solid-wood doors, fiberglass doors should also be inspected closely. They tend to develop little splinters that stick out of the door so that you should not run your hand or finger along the surface to check for them. Be sure to check whether the door is faded or weathered-looking. If they face the hot afternoon sun and driving rains, they fade substantially.

Other Doors

You may also run across a storm door or two. Storm doors go on the outside of another door to help provide protection from the elements. One feature you might check is the damper arm that runs from the door to the door frame to close it automatically.

Make sure it works properly. It should be attached firmly to the frame and the door and it should close the door slowly.

Screen doors are easy to inspect. You simply need to make sure the screen is in good shape – no holes, rips, warps, or missing pieces — and that it is fastened securely to a sturdy frame.

ALL DOORS

You should always take a step back and make sure a door looks good and that it is not cracked, scratched, split, or warped. If there is a window in the door you need to make sure the glass is not cracked or broken. Make sure the locks work properly. The door knob should also be inspected as well as the latching mechanism on the door. Finally, make sure the door is sealed properly. If only part of the door seals correctly then the door frame was installed out of plumb or the door has become warped.

WINDOWS

Types of Windows

There are many different types of windows, but double-hung windows are the most popular type of windows on the market today. Other types of windows include: fixed windows, casement windows, jalousie, awning, horizontal and vertical sliders, and hopper windows.

By the time you are conducting your inspection outside you should have already identified the types of all the windows in the home. If you have not done so, you should go back and review the characteristics of each of the types of windows.

A few window samples. Above left is an example of a casement window. Above right is an example of a double-hung window, and the to the right is an example of a slider window.

INSPECTING THE WINDOWS

Make sure panes are not cracked, broken, or missing. Inspect the frame and the wood around it for rot, unpainted places, or missing caulk between the house and the window frame. Make sure the frame has not pulled loose from the house. If it has, water likely slipped down inside the wall. If the windows are vinyl-clad, you need to check out each corner of the vinyl and make sure it is not loose.

House Inspection Tip #9

Open every window to make sure that they are working and easy to open. Also check the blinds and curtains included in the sale work properly. If not, make a note that you will have to purchase some. Make sure that there is ample lighting for your needs.

12

SIDING

While you are checking out the exterior condition of the windows and doors, you should also inspect the siding. The house you are inspecting can have one of a variety of sidings on it, and there are many types. It is up to you to identify the type of siding: painted wood, board and batten, cedar boards or shingles, hardboard composite, asbestos cement, fiber cement, exterior plywood, vinyl, aluminum, brick, block, or stucco.

Though you will need to make note of the type of siding and inspect it accordingly, look for holes or tears in the siding. Make sure there are no sections that are falling away from the house. Sometimes previous owners will try to cover problems by painting the siding. You may want to carry a tool with you such as an awl (a tool similar to a screw driver but with a pointed steel tip) to help you inspect the wood. Be sure to check where the siding meets anything else such as brick or a chimney. You want to check that there is not a gap where moisture can enter. Check closely where the siding has been drilled for television cables, phone lines or faucets as these holes may let in water.

Many older homes were painted with lead based paint. Lead has been shown to cause developmental and behavioral problems in children.

The main causes for siding problems weather, insects, or poor construction. One problem could be with bees. While inspecting be on the lookout for bees' nests on or near the siding. (Do not disturb them.)

PAINTED WOOD SIDING

Wood siding is painted to protect it and the material behind it from the elements. Look at the condition of the paint for cracking, blistering, or peeling. If you see a problem with the paint, see whether the wood is cracking, swelling, delaminating, or disintegrating. Make sure there is no build-up of mildew particularly where there is no sunlight.

If the siding of the home you are inspecting is painted, it will need new paint regularly. This means that painted wood siding is fairly high-maintenance.

BOARD AND BATTEN SIDING

Board and batten siding is rarely used with newer homes. However, it is more common on older, rural homes. Cedar is the most common type of wood for board and batten siding, but any type of board can be used. You can identify this type of siding because it has wide vertical boards that are separated by smaller boards. The smaller boards are known as "battens."

Board and batten siding can be painted or unpainted. Look for anything that will allow water to enter the house, including missing knotholes and split wood.

CEDAR BOARD OR SHINGLE SIDING

Cedar makes one of the most beautiful sidings and it lasts a long time. It can be installed horizontally or vertically, in the form of shingles, stained, painted, or bare. If the siding is bare, it should turn a silver grey.

Cedar board siding comes in different grades with lowest grades having the largest knots. Make sure that none of the knots are hollowed out. Cedar boards can split and the thinner the board, the easier it will split. Highest quality and best looking cedar boards are usually on the front, and worst looking, lowest quality boards on the back of the house so that you should look closely at the boards on the back. Most likely the back will be where you will find the most problems if you find any problems at all.

Cedar siding can also be shingles or shakes. The shingles are between one and one and a half feet long. They are not thick so they are easily split or broken with age. Look for shingles that are ready to fall off and for spaces where shingles are missing.

If the cedar shingles have been left unpainted or unfinished, make sure they have turned the right color after being weathered. Sometimes the shingles will turn a color that is less than desirable because of dark mold. It affects the color and will cause rot if not addressed. Pay special attention to the corners of the house for discoloring where water may have dripped from the downspouts. Discoloration can also occur at the bottom of the siding where rainwater has splashed up. Over time the wood will be damaged.

Finally, make sure there are no dark streaks running from the nails and down the siding. This is a sign that the wrong type of nail was used to install the siding.

HARDBOARD SIDING

Hardwood siding, also known as hardwood composite siding, is made of bonded wood fibers. You may see any number of surface treatments and textures. It is usually installed in sections that are four feet long and nine or twelve inches wide. The material is fairly dense so it seems durable as a siding, but not so.

Hardboard siding has proved to be unsuccessful in many parts of the country. Because of lawsuits over the material, houses can no longer be built with hardboard siding, but you may still encounter it.

Hardboard siding can swell up if water gets behind the paint because it absorbs water easily. The swelling will be most noticeable where the ends of the boards come together. They will begin to rot soon after swelling occurs. As with most siding, pay particular attention to where the siding meets brick or block and where the siding ends or begins at the corners. Moisture is more likely to enter in these places and cause swelling and rot. Pay attention to where holes have been cut into the siding for wires or pipes. All these holes must be properly sealed or water will get in and cause problems. You may also see bubbles in the paint around where nails have been hammered in to attach the siding. This is another sign that water has got in behind the paint. Also, make sure there is no sign of water penetration where anything, such as a porch railing, has been screwed in or nailed into the siding.

While you are inspecting the hardwood siding, you should stand 30 or 40 feet from the house. The distance will allow you to see problems that may be missed close up. You should look out for any part of the wall that stands out from the rest such as puffed out areas and peeling or blistered paint. You should also inspect the edges for cracking and splitting wood. Be sure to check all sides of the house but check the weathered side of the house closely as it is the side most likely to have defects.

ASBESTOS CEMENT SIDING

Asbestos cement shingles may no longer be manufactured because of health risks it poses. It is still present on many homes. You can recognize it because the shingles are thin and often are scalloped at the bottom. They are usually white or green. They are durable — resistant to weather, rot, and termite infestation. These features make them easy to maintain. However, they are brittle so that they crack if hit. The lower parts of the siding are especially susceptible to damage.

You should look for broken, cracked, loose, or missing shingles. Many times when one shingle slips out of place, other shingles will follow. Asbestos is only considered dangerous when it gets into the air and is then inhaled by humans. Experts agree that the shingles should not be removed. So if you run across asbestos cement siding you want to make a note of it. You will also want to make sure that as a precaution, no children play directly beside the house in case asbestos is in the dirt.

FIBER CEMENT SIDING

Fiber cement siding is similar to asbestos cement siding, but it is safer. It seems to work well. It is always $^5/_{16}$ of an inch thick. The standard length is 12 feet, and the widths range from six to twelve inches. You may also run across fiber cement siding that is actually four feet wide. The two most popular types of fiber cement siding have a wood-grain or smooth surface.

It can be made to look like any other type of siding, installed vertically or horizontally, painted or stained. As with the asbestos cement siding, you should take a screw driver and tap the siding to determine what type it is. If it sounds like a pie plate then it may be fiber cement siding. If you have any question, consult a professional.

The only thing you need to look out for with the fiber cement siding is the possibility that sections of it were cracked during installation. Other than that, this type of siding is supposed to be low maintenance and fire and insect retardant. It is also protected against sun spotting and any other weather related problems.

EXTERIOR PLYWOOD SIDING

While inspecting the paneling on the outside of the house, you may find exterior plywood siding. The plywood panels are usually installed vertically. They usually come in a standard size of four feet wide by eight feet long. The thickness of the panel usually varies between $^3/_8$ inch and $^5/_8$ inch. Exterior plywood siding is easy and inexpensive to install. These two facts are the reason that this type of siding is popular with do-it-yourself homeowners and contractors who are asked to put up siding quickly and inexpensively, but be careful it may have been installed improperly leading to a variety of problems.

The plywood needs to have a healthy coat of paint or sealant to protect it from getting wet and absorbing water. Paint or sealant must be reapplied every few years. If not, the wood begins to bow, delaminate, or becomes damaged quickly. While inspecting the siding, you will be able to tell if it has been damaged by water because you will see that the siding may be alternately concave and convex for the length of the house.

Even if the exterior plywood siding was installed correctly, you still may find the same problems with the siding. You should also pay particular attention to the upper part of each section of siding. If the siding does not have the correct flashing, water may accumulate on the upper edge and cause damage. Also, closely examine the bottom of the siding where rainwater splashes up onto it. Pay special attention to the side of the house that sees the driving rain and the heaviest winds.

VINYL SIDING

Vinyl and aluminum siding are similar. You may need to examine it to tell whether it is vinyl or aluminum. The coloring of vinyl siding is actually imbedded in the material and runs throughout the thickness of the siding. The coloring for aluminum siding is only on the surface. So, when you analyze the end of the siding, if you see that the siding is completely colored then it is vinyl siding. If the coloring is only on the surface, it is aluminum.

Inspect it for any cracked or broken sections. Usually it will not dent as it springs back when impacted, but during cold weather it can become brittle and will crack or break if it is hit hard enough.

It also expands and contracts as the temperature changes. If it was improperly installed, it may blister or become wavy.

ALUMINUM SIDING

As was mentioned above, aluminum siding looks similar to vinyl siding. Check the coloring (details above) to determine which it is. Aluminum siding is becoming less and less popular as most new homes are now being built or remodeled with vinyl siding. It looks good for years, although it scratches and dents easily. Check whether any sections have been ripped away from the house.

BRICK EXTERIOR

Brick lasts a long time, and it is easy to maintain. Solid brick is just what it sounds like: a wall that provides the structural support for the building as well as being the finished exterior wall.

Check a brick exterior to see whether it may be brick veneer that will have a stud wall to provide structural support. The brick veneer is just a thin wall of bricks built on the outer side of the stud wall. You can usually tell which type you are inspecting by looking above and around the windows and doors. Brick veneer has the same pattern that continues around the windows and doorways. If it is solid brick, you will see that the pattern changes around windows and doors as most masons build in an arch above windows and doorways.

Brick will not last forever if they were not properly installed. Make sure you inspect every wall closely. Look for Z-shaped cracks that indicate the footer has settled. Do not be concerned with a few small cracks, but if all the cracks join together, there is a problem with the footer.

While inspecting the brick walls, you should also look for broken bricks and crumbling or missing mortar joints. Use an awl to poke at the mortar to see how solid it is.

It should be easy for you to spot any missing mortar joints. It will be more difficult to find bricks that are breaking apart or crumbling. You are most likely to find problem on the side of the house that faces the prevailing wind and on corners in locales that freeze in winter. Also check for lighter color of bricks that have lost their facing.

BLOCKS

Block is an outside wall. It is sturdy, easy to maintain, and it lasts a long time. You may see block that has a stone veneer over it, or you may find blocks that have an attractive finish on them. No matter what the block wall may look like, it will be quite easy to inspect.

If the building is fairly new, you probably only want to check for major cracks. As with the brick, you also want to check for Z-shaped cracks that may indicate a problem with the footer. For older buildings, you will want to probe the mortar in between

the blocks with your awl. You also want to inspect the corners to make sure the blocks there are not falling apart. Finally, though it is relatively easy to correct, check to make sure there is no mildew on the blocks.

STUCCO

There are three main types of stucco siding: synthetic, hard coat, and a combination of both. If you happen to know the type of stucco, you are aware that hard coat stucco siding leaks water causing the insides of the walls to rot out. Even more of the synthetic stucco siding has this problem.

Stucco siding that is not properly installed can let in moisture and not show any signs of damage. However, the joists and framing members will be rotting on the inside while from the outside everything looks fine. Inspect the stucco siding for cracks. Most stucco has some cracks in it. Also, look for other places where water can get behind the siding.

If the stucco siding is synthetic, there may also be a problem with termites and carpenter ants if it is less than a half foot off the ground. If you see the stucco is close to the ground, note that there is potential for an insect infestation.

It is not easy to determine if there is any leaking or rotting behind the stucco siding. There are instruments that you can buy that will tell you, but they are expensive and difficult to use. You should just note all the normal problems that you can: cracks, peeling paint, holes, missing flashing, rotted wood, and stains. Then recommend that the stucco siding be checked out by someone who is an expert in it.

House Inspection Tip #10

Pay as close attention to the exterior of the house as the interior. Look on the siding of the house to check if the paint is in good condition or if there are any cracks in the siding. Are there signs of rotting trim? Are the gutters clogged or coming loose?

13

FOUNDATION & DECKS

Next are the foundation and any decks. The foundation supports the home, and the decks have a support system to support the deck.

Do not forget to review over the CD-ROM for forms and checklists for use when inspecting a potential home.

FOUNDATIONS

The job of the foundation is to support the house. Most foundations are made up of walls that are supported by a larger base called a footing. Normally the footing is resting on soil that has not been disturbed. In climates where the ground freezes, the footing must be located beneath the frost line. Piers, columns, and pilasters may also be employed to help support the house.

The house is anchored to the foundation so that it does not shift or move when a strong wind pushes against it. It also helps keep the house stationary in the event of an earthquake or any other trauma to the house or the ground surrounding it. There are also natural forces from the ground's pressure that push the foundation besides the weight of the home. The foundation walls must deal with all this stress. If there is a question about whether the foundation can withstand all the stress, pilasters are usually installed to help give the foundation extra strength.

SOLID FOUNDATIONS

While you were in the basement you should have already noticed whether the walls were in good condition. Solid foundations have a skirt that runs continuously around the house.

The solid foundation can be made of almost any type of material: wood, brick, rock, block, or poured concrete. The material simply has to run from the footer all the way up to the framing. Many older homes may have a rock foundation that was collected from the fields surrounding the home. While the rock may last forever, the seals will not. Use your awl to make sure there are no gaps between the rock and the foundation beams that the rock is supporting.

Block foundations are usually pretty solid. The only way they pose a problem is if the footer has a defect. As we mentioned with the block siding in the previous chapter, check the foundation walls for Z-shaped cracks. Brick foundations are vulnerable to the same problems as the block foundations.

PIERS AND COLUMNS

Not every house has a foundation that runs entire length of the house. Some homes have supports that are placed at regular intervals so that the house is supported adequately. These types of foundations are called piers and columns. The foundation can be made of rock, brick, wood, block, steel, or concrete. If you are inspecting a home near the coast, on a steep hill, or over loose soil, you may well see circular concrete pillars and giant poles supporting the building.

LOW FOUNDATIONS

Every house must have a foundation but on some homes it rests below ground level, meaning that the floor joists are actually sitting on the ground. This is especially common with houses that were built around 1900 or so. Back then a person believed wood was too hard to rot in a short amount of time. They were right. The wood did not rot in their lifetime.

CONDITION OF THE FOUNDATION

Solid foundations made of block or brick need to be inspected

for Z-shaped cracks. You should look for major cracks and a series of smaller cracks that run together. The constant pressure of the earth pushing against the foundation may cause it to bow inward. For the brick foundation you also need to check the condition of the  bricks and mortar. Use your awl to scratch the mortar because some cracks are under the surface.

As was discussed in the previous chapter, you need to be

particularly careful if stucco is involved. In this case, if stucco is covering the foundation or any other material is covering it, you have to inspect carefully for signs of water damage. Be aware that many times stucco or a similar covering is sometimes used to cover up defects on the outer wall. Be sure to inspect the inside of the wall for any evidence of water damage that may be occurring on the outside of the foundation.

If the foundation consists of piers and columns, you need to check for a whole different set of potential problems. If the piers or columns are made of rock, steel, block, or concrete, you do not have to worry about deterioration. However, wood and brick can deteriorate over time. Therefore, inspect wood and brick foundations. Also, sometimes wood is used to help fill a gap between a more solid foundation (like rock) and the structure of the house. Be sure to check the length of the foundation to make sure the house is resting solidly on it. Sometimes the wood that was used to fill the gap has broken down and fallen out, and the house is left with no foundation.

Any time there is a material used that is susceptible to rot or decay you should inspect it carefully and thoroughly for cracks and mildew. Pay special attention to posts or columns that are partially hidden in brush and make sure you always check for rot and decay a few inches below the surface of the ground. In areas that tend to flood or even in parts of the foundation where water collects, posts will rot quickly. Look for mud rings to tell whether water has a tendency to accumulate around posts.

For low foundations, you want to make sure the floor joists are not resting against or in the soil causing them to rot quickly. If you noticed that the floor was sagging when you were inside and the floor joists are on or in the ground, the joists are rotten. If you did not notice that the floor was sagging but the floor joists are too low, you may want to go back inside and re-inspect the floor to see whether it is indeed sagging.

If the foundation is only a crawl space, you may have a problem with rotting floor joists even if they are above the ground. Check to make sure the crawl space is properly vented. If there are no vents, chances are that the joists are or soon will be rotting.

One final thing to inspect is the skirt-board that runs along the bottom of the house. If that board is in poor shape, the support beams on the other side of it are probably in bad shape as well. Be aware that a new skirt-board may also indicate trouble with the support beams. Many sellers will replace the skirt-beam in hopes that they can cover up the problem with the support beams and sell their house quickly.

TERMITES AND OTHER INFESTATIONS

You need to be aware of and look for possible signs of termite infestation. If you find a colony of termites it usually takes years for them to do major damage to a house. To find them, inspect all exposed wood from the attic to the basement. Check all outside wood that is close to or touching the ground. Probe wood that is vulnerable to infestation such as basement windowsills and frames, deck posts, and the bottom of garage doors. You should also probe sections of wood that are near concrete-covered, soil-filled porches as well as fences, dead trees, or stacked wood. If you are not sure how much damage the termites have done to the house, you should ask for help from a professional.

In certain parts of the country you may find other harmful infestations, including carpenter ants and powder-post beetles.

Ants may actually be visible in and around the house. Look for small piles of sawdust and rotten areas in wood. You may hear something that sounds like crackling paper if you stand near a carpenter ant nest. With powder-post beetles, you should notice clusters of small round holes in the wood framing. Probe them for signs of deterioration or infestation.

DECKS

The problem with decks is that many times homeowners will install them themselves which usually results in their being built poorly.

Deck Surface

You may find violations of codes and common sense. When you look at the deck, make sure there are no obvious problems. For example, if the deck is not completely covered by the roof, make

sure there is a gutter that stops rain from running off the roof directly onto the deck surface. Check the deck surface for rotten boards. Make sure you are able to walk on them and on the steps safely. You should inspect the parts of the deck that are under trees and susceptible to algae growth. Algae will make the deck deteriorate faster and it will also cause hazardous slippery spots.

Find out how old the deck is. Even decks that have been properly constructed and installed with treated wood will eventually deteriorate and need to be replaced. However, decks that have been built with treated wood should last at least 10 years or longer, depending on the climate and maintenance.

Even treated wood needs to be protected from water penetration. Decks that have been neglected will suffer water damage and

have their grey grain coming right out of the wood. Boards may appear permanently dark and wet. Be sure to check the edge of the boards for the start of warping.

The final thing you should check on the deck surface is the nails or screws that fasten down the boards. The best way to fasten down the boards is with stainless steel screws. Look for nails or screws emerging from the deck surface, meaning the wrong nails or screws were used to fasten down the boards. Changes in temperature may also cause nails or screws to pop out above the

surface. While they may not seem like much, all you have to do is trip on one or catch a bare foot on it and you will know that it is indeed a big deal.

Deck Railings

Local building codes may require that any deck must have a railing around it. Most codes require one but even if your local codes do not, you should see that a sturdy rail is put in place. Check for any signs of rotting or insect infestation.

Vertical supports that run from the rail to the deck surface are as important as the railing itself and so is the amount of space between each of the vertical supports. To make sure no one falls through or gets stuck in between the supports, they should be no farther apart than four inches. Be sure to check that none of the vertical supports is loose or missing.

Support Posts

When you check the support posts, make sure that all of them are where they should be. Next look at each post to make sure it is in good condition. The two most common types of support posts are masonry and treated wood. Make sure masonry posts do not have any broken bricks or blocks and that the mortar is in good shape. Treated wood posts need to be checked for major cracks and warping. You also need to make sure the posts are bolted to the deck surface.

Support posts should have some type of concrete base or

another type of footer on them to prevent them from sinking into the ground. Without a footer or base, the deck will usually slope badly. (A slight slope going down away from the house is actually a good thing to have so that rainwater drains off the deck.) Finally, the deck should either be free from the house or it should be securely bolted to the house.

House Inspection Tip #11

It is vital that you carefully check the house foundation for any visible cracks. Cracks over $1/8$" or cracks that are mis-aligned are a potential warning sign. Also make sure that the foundation is high enough off the ground so insects cannot easily come inside.

14

THE GARAGE

While you are performing your inspection outside, look at the garage. There are two basic types of garages: attached and detached. Detached garages can be broken down into two subcategories: detached and detached with a breezeway or a porch. Attached garages are connected to the house; they may have a part of the home above them or they may be on the side of the house. A detached garage is separated from the house and may be right next to it or across an alley, for example.

DETACHED GARAGE

One of the advantages of a detached garage is that it is safer than attached garages especially if a fire starts there. (Vehicles, particularly certain trucks, have been known to combust spontaneously.) A disadvantage is that the structure may not be as sturdy or sound as it should be. Also, if the home is located in a colder climate, drivers will have to go outside to get to their car.

INSPECTING THE EXTERIOR

You should inspect the outside of the garage the same way you looked at the outside of the home. Look at the walls, windows, and doors. Check the siding for any potential problems. Remember that the siding should end well before it touches the ground. If the siding goes too low, the garage may be infested with termites or carpenter ants. All the other problems that houses may experience with siding also apply to garages. Pay particular attention to the back wall of the garage. Inspect it carefully for any signs that it may have been hit by a car from inside.

Look at the windows and doors to make sure they are in decent shape. Again, the same rules for inspecting the house's windows and doors apply to these windows and doors. It is up to the potential homeowner to decide how important the detached garage's condition is.

Check the roof and the gutters for any flaws. The gutter should be securely fastened to the building and not missing any sections, and the downspouts should work. If the roof extends out from the building, there may not be any gutters present. The roof should not be sagging in any way. Check it with binoculars and make sure it is in decent shape. For more information about inspecting roofs, see the next chapter (Chapter 15).

INSPECTING THE INTERIOR

Look up and make sure the roof looks solid from the inside. You should not be able to see any daylight coming through cracks. Check for water stains on the inside woodwork for any past leaks. Look at the walls for cracks or signs of crumbling. Inspect any exposed studs as well for cracks, breaks, or eaten away by termites.

The floor may be dirt, concrete, or asphalt. The condition of the floor will indicate whether the floor was installed correctly and provide clues as to the quality of the workmanship on the rest of the garage. If the floor is dirt, you may have problems in the future. When the dirt gets damp, it will rot the wood and cause any metal in the garage to rust.

Check the garage door to make sure it operates correctly. If it is electric, you should open and close it a couple of times, checking to make sure there is a safety feature that will stop the door from closing if something or someone gets in the way. If this feature is not present, make a  note of it. If the door opens and closes manually, make sure it slides easily and that it stays up when open. You do not want the door to crash down on someone or on a car!

Make sure any heaters work by turning up the thermostat. If the heater is not electric, you need to make sure it is properly vented to the outside. If it is not, ask for proof that it does not need to be vented to the outside. If it is vented to the outside, make sure the flue does not directly contact the wood frame — a fire hazard.

It is ideal to have power in the garage with at least one three-prong electrical outlet and an overhead light. If the garage is more than a few steps from the house, it would also be ideal to have lights leading the way to the garage. If you see any potential problems with the electricity, consult a professional.

ATTACHED GARAGE

The best thing about attached garages is the convenience. You do not have to walk outside to get into your car, but the major drawback is the possibility of fire starting in the garage and spreading to the main part of the house, especially dangerous with garages that have living areas above them. The garage and the main part of the house should be separated by a fire proof door. Also, any living area should be on a higher level than the garage: there should be at least one step going up from the garage into the main part of house. Anytime the living area is below or even with the garage floor, there is the potential for toxic exhaust and gasoline vapors to enter the house whenever the door is open. The door should also be self-closing to prevent it from making the house susceptible to fumes and fire. (Most houses do not have automatic closing doors, but they should.)

Walls should not be made of wood, but should be filled with insulation and covered with some type of fireproof coating. If there is a living area above the garage, the ceiling of the garage should have a fire resistant coating and contain insulation.

Sometimes the garage is located below the entire living area along with the basement. If this is the case, the furnace should be as far away as possible. If the car's gas tank develops a leak and if the garage or basement is not properly ventilated, the fumes will ignite when the furnace fires.

Another potential hazard is an entrance to the attic being above the garage. If so, make sure the hatch cover is over the attic opening because if a fire breaks out in the garage, the hole leading up into the attic will suck the flames right up through the hole and into the attic and spread through the entire house fast. Make sure the hatch cover is always in place.

You should also check the ceiling to make sure there are no stains from leaks in plumbing. Close the garage door so that you can see the entire ceiling. If you see stains, check whatever is above the ceiling and inspect that part of the plumbing again to make sure there are no current leaks. If there are exposed drains or pipes in the garage and the house is located in a colder climate, the pipes should be insulated against freezing.

Look at the wall for signs of damage and rot. Check the floor as well for signs of water damage and termite infestation. If there is a heat register or a radiator, make sure it works. If the heat is warm air, make sure there are no return air ducts as they will pull poisonous gases into the house.

House Inspection Tip #12

Treat the garage as another room on the house. Make sure that there are no cracks in the floor and check all electrical outlets. Check all doors, not just the car entryway, to make sure they work. Make sure all windows inside the garage are fully functional.

15

THE ROOF

A faulty roof can cost you a great deal of money. A good way to inspect the house is by using a pair of binoculars to double-check areas above any signs of leaking that you found in the attic. The main types of roofs are asphalt shingles, wood shingles, shakes, slate, tile, and standing seam. This chapter will first explain how to perform the walk-about inspection and then it will detail the characteristics of each type of roof and what kind of problems to check out.

WALK-ABOUT INSPECTION

The way to perform the walk-about inspection is to walk around the house looking at every inch of the roof through a pair of binoculars. Obvious problems such as missing tiles or shingles, and holes in the roof, will be discussed when each type of roof is explained later in this chapter.

When you look at the roof, the first thing you should notice is the entire length of the peak of the roof, which should be ruler-straight without sags or bends. If it is not even, the problem is a rotting or cracked ridge beam. If the peak is wavy, most likely the sheathing of the roof is too thin, or it is delaminating or rotting. On older homes too many layers of shingles can cause a roof to look wavy because the roof is too weak to support the weight of the shingles.

Remember to look at the gutters as you perform the walk-about inspection. You should also inspect the soffits, fascia boards, and the rake boards. Make sure none is rotting, dislodging, or pocked.

Check the area around anything that sticks up out of the roof: chimneys, skylights, attic, plumbing, and gas vents. Make sure flashing is present and in good shape. Flashing often fails, and it is difficult to tell from the outside whether it is still working properly. You would have detected any flashing failures while you were inspecting the inside of the home. If not, you should re-inspect those areas.

You should also closely inspect any skylights that stick-up out of the roof. You should have already checked beneath and around the skylights while you were performing the inside inspection. If not, make sure you go back and inspect the appropriate areas around the skylights.

You should also pay particular attention to any place where two separate roofs meet, a usual place for leaks.

ASPHALT SHINGLES

Asphalt shingles, also known as laminated or composition shingles, are the most common type of roof covering. Their biggest advantage is that they can be reapplied over each other as needed. Most states will allow up to three layers to be applied on a roof. Occasionally the three layers will create too much weight and the roof will sag. As the inspector, you need to note this problem.

There are two basic types of asphalt shingles, organic or fiberglass-based. All shingles deteriorate over time, but organic asphalt shingles tend to cup, curl, crack, blister, rot, buckle, disintegrate, or completely break apart. Deterioration can be accelerated by heat build-up in the attic. The side of the roof that gets the most sunlight will break down first. They deteriorate faster in warmer climates.

While you have the binoculars, look for any nails that might be popping up out of the shingles. They will allow shingles to curl and be blown away.

Blistering occurs when water penetrates the upper layer, causing bubbles and sometimes breakage in the middle of the shingle. Rotting begins with the shingles' curling at the edges Curling also occurs when the backing is too weak to hold the entire shingle in place, a result of age and heat. All three of these problems will allow water to get under the surface of the roof.

You should also look for roof patches and missing or loose shingles. Fiberglass shingles are more likely to come loose and blow away because they are lightweight and do not stick to each other. Make a note of any torn or ripped shingles. Check for green algae growing beneath the roof and siding and for moss growing on top the shingles. If they are not removed, they will rot the shingles.

WOOD SHAKES AND SHINGLES

Wood shakes are much rougher looking than wood shingles. Both may be made of cedar, Southern pine, redwood, or many other less popular types of wood. Wood shakes and shingles look beautiful, but they are temporary. When inspecting them, look  for any signs of broken, cracked, or rotten wooden shakes and shingles. If so, the roof is overdue for leaking.

Never attempt to walk on wood roof coverings because they can be slippery. There is a higher risk for fires when the roof is made out of wood. You should ask the owner for proof that the shakes or shingles have been treated to resist fire. Finally, under certain conditions cedar shakes have been known to dissolve and disappear. While they are in the process of dissolving they will appear to be getting thinner and tapered and they will develop holes.

SLATE

Slate roofs are made of a dense, hard rock that is cut thin. They are uncommon, durable, water resistant, and fire proof, but they are high maintenance because their corners can break off or an entire slate can split. If a lesser quality slate, called ribbon slate, is used, there will be far more problems. Ribbons in the slate are softer than normal slate so it will crack along the ribbons. Check for any patches on the roof, probably made of asphalt cement, which sometimes dries out and cracks so that it needs to be reapplied regularly.

TILE

There really is not too much to inspect with tile roofing. You only need to be concerned with cracked or missing tiles. They usually fade, affecting the overall appearance of the roof but not the quality.

STANDING SEAM

Standing seam roofs were most popular in the beginning of the 1900s. Recently they have made a comeback. They come in rolls of stainless steel, copper, tin, or steel plate (terneplate), either 20 or 24 inches wide and 50 feet long that can be cut to fit the house. Aluminum sheets should not be confused with standing seam. You can tell the difference because aluminum sheets have a V-shape bent into them (to help with support) and they are produced in shorter sections than standing seam.

Standing seam roofs last a long time. One reason is that they do not require nails so there is no threat of water seeping into the nail holes.

In certain parts of the country the standing seam roofing is said to last 100 years. When you inspect standing seam roofing, you should look for areas of rust that are darker-colored spots or streaks of reddish-colored stripes. Areas around aluminum flashing will rust out before any other part of the standing seam roofing.

GUTTERING AND DOWNSPOUTS

Gutters collect rain from the roof and direct it to the ground via downspouts. Without them, rain would run off the house, causing erosion or basement flooding. Make sure that the gutters work and that the downspouts are connected and free of obstructions. Sometimes you will actually see plants or small trees growing from the gutters.

There are two basic types of gutters: built-in gutters and exterior-mounted gutters.

Built-In Gutters

Built-in gutters are not common. They are part of the house that extends from the roof, and they require occasional maintenance. A leaky gutter causes the soffit to rot.

Exterior-Mounted Gutters

This type of gutter can be made of copper (the most expensive), galvanized iron, wood, aluminum (the most common), or plastic. Galvanized iron gutters are inexpensive, but they corrode easily and require frequent maintenance. Aluminum gutters are a popular alternative because they are also inexpensive, and they do not corrode. Wood gutters often crack or rot. They need to be maintained with a new coat of paint and inside coating the gutter every few years. Plastic gutters have not been widely accepted, but you may see them on a house.

You should always check the gutters, paying special attention to the seams and the connections to the downspouts. Using binoculars, look at every inch of the gutter to make sure that it is firmly attached with no sagging or missing sections.

Downspouts

The main thing you need to check with downspouts is that they are present in good enough numbers for the size of the house. If there are too few, rainwater will overflow the gutters, making them useless. Make sure that each downspout is firmly attached and carries water far enough away from the house. Obviously you do not want a downspout pouring water into the side of a hill where it will simply flow back to the house. Trace with your eyes where the water from each downspout will go so that you know you will not have the water flooding the basement.

House Inspection Tip #13

A roof can be extremely costly to replace, so make sure you give it a thorough inspection. See if there is any sagging or rotting. Make sure to find out how long it has been since the roof has been replaced, and factor in how long it will be until it needs replacement.

16

THE SURROUNDING AREA

Anything that might be on the outside of the home or surrounding the home will be covered in this chapter: driveways, walkways and sidewalks, patios, grading/water drainage, landscaping, swimming pools, and any out buildings not including detached garages.

DRIVEWAYS

Some people are picky about the condition of the driveway while others do not even look at it when deciding whether to purchase a house. Make sure it is wide enough, in good shape, and that the location and the design will work for you.

The three basic types of driveways are concrete/asphalt, gravel, and dirt. Gravel and dirt driveways are common in rural areas and may develop holes and ruts over time. Gravel driveways require fresh gravel occasionally. Almost all driveways in urban areas will be either concrete or asphalt, which should be inspected for cracks or breaks. If it is breaking apart, you may need to replace the entire surface.

A driveway should be at least eight feet wide. If the house is on a busy street, a built-in turnaround spot as part of the driveway would avoid a potentially dangerous entry to the street.

Check to see if the driveway is level. If it slopes down toward the house, the house and the garage are vulnerable to flooding. All the rainwater will run directly down the hill and into the house unless there is a channel drain that runs across the driveway. This channel drain should take all the water running down the driveway and direct it elsewhere. Ideally, water runs to a drain that has a free-flowing outlet for water. If the drain sends the water to a basin, it may fill when the water table is high, making the channel drain useless. If the driveway is located on a sloping street, you should inspect the curb where the driveway meets the street. The curb should not be cut level with the street. You want there to be a small ridge so that any water flowing down the street does not flow into your driveway.

While standing at the end of the driveway, look up and down the street for any trees, bushes, shrubs, or any other obstruction that might block a person's vision when exiting the driveway.

If the house is located where winters are icy and snowy, you want to pay attention to the slope on the driveway because you will be driving up and down it all winter.

WALKWAYS AND SIDEWALKS

Walkways and sidewalks are usually made from concrete, asphalt, or stone that is sunk into the earth. Inspect them the same way you inspect a driveway. Note any large cracks or raised sections. If someone comes along, trips, and suffers injuries, or pretends to be injured, the owner may be liable.

PATIOS

Some patios are made with wood imbedded in the ground between either concrete or brick which should be checked for rot and possibly treated. Concrete slabs should have some type of expansion and control joints to help prevent cracks in the patio.

Patios should be sloped away from the house for water drainage. If the patio slopes toward the house, report it and check that no water is getting into the basement next to the patio. Some patios are not sloped at all. You may notice gravel or some other covering between the patio and the house, insinuating that there is a drainage system in place below. Make sure that the gravel is not merely camouflage.

BALCONIES

Most balconies are extensions of the house; that is, all their support comes from the house. If you see a balcony with support beams, make sure the beams are connected to a footer and are not cracked, broken, or rotting. If there are no support beams, pay particular attention to the part of the balcony that connects to the house. A problem here could destroy your balcony and cause massive damage to the house itself.

Just as you checked the railings on porches, you should also check the "wiggle" on the railing to ensure that no one will fall off. Make sure the railing is at an appropriate height and is firmly attached to the balcony.

GRADING/WATER DRAINAGE

A house that has never had any problems with drainage may suddenly develop a problem—a major headache for any homeowner. It could be due to land development nearby, such as shopping malls and office parks that cause rainwater to flow into the backyards of unsuspecting homeowners. This is an example of a bad situation that a future homeowner could easily ignore when deciding to purchase a home.

The topography around the house can make a difference in its value — whether it is located on a hill with a steep driveway or below the level of the street and whether it is in a flood zone or beside a creek that could overflow in the spring.

Be sure to note if the house is located in a low-lying area. Check the grading around the house for signs that flooding may have occurred. Do not assume that the house is not in a flood zone. One clue is whether the present homeowner has been required to buy flood insurance. It is a mistake to think that because a house is in the city or in an urban area that it cannot be at flood risk. This is not true. In fact, all the rainwater from the neighborhood has to flow somewhere. If the neighborhood does not have adequate storm drains, all that rainwater may well flow right into your lawn or back up through your basement drain.

If the house is located at the bottom of a hill you should try to figure out how rainwater running off the hill is getting around the house. There may be an underground drain running alongside the footer of the house to take water away. You will not be able to see it; therefore you need to check for signs of water damage in the basement and around the house. New basement wall coverings may be a clue that there is a major problem. It is not beyond an eager seller to patch or cover up a wall temporarily, perhaps behind basement steps where you would never suspect a problem unless you have noted that water would naturally flow in from that direction.

The point is that just because you do not find any water damage to the house or in the basement does not mean there is not a grading problem that needs to be fixed. Water could be flowing toward the house and then under it to compromise the supports for the house causing ruinous structural damage.

LANDSCAPING

You cannot judge a house by its landscaping, which may be gorgeous, but the house is in poor condition and vice versa. Look closely at the lawn, trees, shrubs, and any other improvements such as flower gardens and waterfalls.

THE LAWN

Many people only see the value of a lawn in its beauty, but a lawn prevents topsoil from eroding. Weeds and crabgrass can be turned into a perfect lawn, if that is important to you.

Moles can ruin the looks of the lawn by burrowing into the ground, leaving little holes, and creating little mounds of dirt (mole hills). They are not difficult to exterminate.

You may also find sunken spots and holes on the lawn. They should be filled in with dirt so they are no risk for people walking across the lawn. You should inspect the entire lawn to see if there are any areas that are extremely sloped. If a person tries to mow a steep area with a riding mower, the mower may turn over and cause serious injury. Even if the lawn is mowed with a push-mower, a person could slip on the incline and contact the revolving blade.

Finally, if you are inspecting a home that was just built and there is not yet a lawn, you better find out who is responsible for starting a new lawn. If it is you, the cost could be so expensive that you have second thoughts about buying the house.

SHRUBS

A seller may plant new shrubs to improve the overall appearance of the home, but if they are planted close together so that they look good immediately, they may grow much larger and cover walkways or die from overcrowding. Pruning or removal is the answer.

TREES

Inspect trees that are close to the house or wherever people will be walking or sitting. Hanging limbs are dangerous because they could fall on a person, the house, a car, or some other valuable asset. Dead trees could also fall and damage property.

If trees are deciduous and it is winter, you may need to hire a professional to tell you the general health of all the trees near the house. Taking out large, dead trees is expensive, but if you decide to do it, hire a professional who has insurance in case any damage to the property occurs during removal.

FENCES

Depending on their length, fences on a property are generally not costly to repair. However, you should inspect their condition. You may find that a fence is in such poor shape that it needs to be replaced or removed.

Wooden fences should be closely inspected for signs of rot, termites, breaks, cracks, or missing sections. Check gates the same way you inspect the rest of the fence and make sure they work properly.

Check a metal fence for rust and for any loose or broken sections. Most chain link fences are made of galvanized steel. There are two ways to galvanize steel, electroplating and hot dipping. Electroplating produces a thin coat of protection that does not always prevent rust so that the fence requires occasional maintenance. Hot-dipping the steel produces a nice heavy coat good for keeping rust at bay. A vinyl coating keeps the fence rust free, and will last a long time.

In the next section we will discuss swimming pools, but any swimming pool should be surrounded by a fence of some sort. Check the local ordinance requirements as to height and acceptable materials. Even if there is no ordinance requiring a fence, it is always a good idea to have one anyway. You certainly do not want a child or even an animal wandering into your pool and drowning.

SWIMMING POOLS

A pool in poor condition can be a major source of stress from expense and danger.

Types of Swimming Pools

There are three basic types of swimming pools: concrete, vinyl-lined, and preformed fiberglass pools.

There are four methods for installing a concrete pool:

- poured concrete
- concrete block
- shotcrete
- gunite

Regardless of the method used to construct it, a waterproof shell must be placed over the concrete so that the pool will hold water. Most concrete pools are finished with plaster, which provides a smooth, non-skid surface that will last more than ten years, depending on maintenance. Another possible sealant is ceramic tile, a great alternative for both performance and appearance, but it is expensive. Two other possible finishes are fiberglass coating and paint. If the pool is painted, think twice about buying the house because maintenance will be ruinous. Paint does not last and you need to sandblast it to remove it.

The top edge of a pool is called coping, and it stops water from getting in behind the shell of the pool. The concrete can serve as the coping if it is extended up past the shell of the pool. Other possible forms of coping are flagstones, bricks, or pre-cast coping stones.

Vinyl-Lined Pools

Vinyl-lined pools are the most inexpensive pools on the market today. There are two main steps to completing the construction of a vinyl-lined pool. First the outside of the pool must be built and then a liner is installed. Most liners are guaranteed to last about ten years. Vinyl lining is used in the construction of above ground pools as well.

Preformed Fiberglass Pools

Preformed fiberglass pools are trucked to their destination and lowered into a perfectly sized hole using a crane. Preformed fiberglass pools have a number of benefits.

- It takes little time to install them because they do not have to be built on site.

- They are extremely tough and durable.

- They are easy to clean because the sides are so smooth that algae have a difficult time clinging to them.

- Once the preformed fiberglass pool is completely installed, it is difficult to tell the difference between the preformed pool and a pool that was constructed at the site.

Inspecting the Swimming Pool

Your first task is to ask the owner if he or she has a permit for the pool. Most places require that the pool be inspected and approved before use. You need to be sure everything is legal before you begin your actual inspection.

While you are asking the owner for the certificate, you should also request the latest maintenance report. If it is not available, ask the owner to submit a written guarantee that the pool and all its parts are in working order.

Normally pools lose water through evaporation, splashing, and by swimmers carrying water out on their bodies. Except for swimmers' splashing, a pool normally loses about an inch of water a month. If more water is being lost during pool season, there is probably a leak in the lining.

The next thing you should is inspect the fence. Again, if the pool is built above the ground no fence may be necessary. However, any pool that is below ground should have a fence even if it is not required by law. Make sure that the fence is in good condition (see the fences section earlier in this chapter) and that it has a working gate and latch. The gate should be self-closing and the latch on the gate should work.

Inspect the area around the pool. There will usually be some type of deck. Most in-ground pools have a concrete deck, while above-ground pool decks usually are made of wood. This chapter has already covered how to inspect different types of decks and patios. You may need to review to inspect the pool's deck.

Inspect accessories for the pool, including the cover, diving boards or platforms, ladders, slides, and grab rails. Have a professional check electric equipment, motors, and pipes for any irregularities. Take into account that regular pool maintenance is costly.

The main job of the pool cover is to keep dirt and other debris out of the pool. It may be used as an extra safety feature to keep children from falling into the pool. If there is a cover on the pool, check it for damage. Is the pool cover strapped down? If so, are any of the straps torn or missing? Make a note of anything that is not right.

Make sure ladders, hand rails, diving board, and the slide are securely attached to the deck. Make sure the board has no cracks and has a non-slip finish.

OTHER BUILDINGS

Out buildings, such as storage sheds, should be inspected the same way you did the house and the garage. Pay attention to any signs of a leaking roof on the inside, and on the inside and outside look for any damage.

APPENDIX A

INSPECTING THE INSIDE OF A HOME CHECKLIST ONE

Part A — Floors

☐ Problems? (Creaking, Squeaking, Sags, Slopes)
Rooms_____

☐ Problems? (Creaking, Squeaking, Sags, Slopes)
Rooms_____

☐ Problems? (Creaking, Squeaking, Sags, Slopes)
Rooms_____

☐ There are soft patches in the _____
located in the _____ part of the room.

☐ Hardwood floors under the carpet in the _____.
Condition? _____.
  ☐ Visual Proof ☐ Signed Representation From Owner

Additional Notes:_____
_____
_____

Part B — Walls

☐ Problems? (Cracks, Bulges, Water Stains, Holes, and Peeling Paint)
Location-_____
☐ Bearing ☐ Non-Bearing

☐ Problems? (Cracks, Bulges, Water Stains, Holes, and Peeling Paint)
Location-_____
☐ Bearing ☐ Non-Bearing

☐ Problems? (Cracks, Bulges, Water Stains, Holes, and Peeling Paint)
Location-_____
☐ Bearing ☐ Non-Bearing

Additional Notes:_____
_____
_____
_____

Part C — Ceilings

☐ Problems? (Peeling, Cracking, Water Stains)
Rooms:_____

☐ Problems? (Peeling, Cracking, Water Stains)
Rooms:_____

☐ Problems? (Peeling, Cracking, Water Stains)
Rooms:_____

Part C — Ceilings

☐ Problems? (Peeling, Cracking, Water Stains)
  Rooms:_____

☐ Larger Problems? (Sagging, Bulging)
  Rooms:_____

☐ Larger Problems? (Sagging, Bulging)
  Rooms:_____

Additional Notes:_____
_____
_____

Part D — Windows

☐ Screens
  ☐ Missing Screens: _____
  ☐ Damaged Screens: _____

☐ Storm Windows
  ☐ Damaged Storm Windows: _____

Types of Windows:

☐ Double-Hung Windows   ☐ Fixed Windows
☐ Casement Windows   ☐ Jalousie
☐ Horizontal and Vertical Sliders ☐ Awning
☐ Fixed Windows   ☐ Other:_____

Part D — Windows

☐   Problems With Windows

Location: _____

Problem: _____

☐   Problems With Windows

Location: _____

Problem: _____

☐   Problems With Windows

Location: _____

Problem: _____

Additional Notes: _____

_____

_____

Part E — Doors

Location / Type of Door	Condition:
_____	_____
	_____
_____	_____
	_____
_____	_____
	_____

Part E — Doors

Number of Interior Doors: _____

Problems With Doors: _____

_____

_____   _____

Additional Notes:_____

_____

_____

Part F — Outlets & Lighting Fixtures

Sufficient Number of Outlets: ☐ Yes   ☐ No

Rooms Needing Additional Outlets: _____

_____

Kitchen & Bathroom Outlets: _____
    Check for GFCI: ☐ Yes   ☐ No

Outlets in Rest of House: _____

Lighting Fixtures In House: _____

_____

Additional Notes:_____

_____

_____

_____

Part G— Heat Registers / Radiators

Type of Heat: _____

_____

Zone Heating: ☐ Yes ☐ No

Outlets in Rest of House: _____

Location of Registers / Radiators: _____

_____

Condition of Registers / Radiators: _____

_____

Area / Space Heaters? ☐ Yes ☐ No
Location:_____

_____

Condition: _____

_____

Additional Notes:_____

_____

_____

_____

_____

CHECKLIST TWO: THE KITCHEN

The Kitchen Sink

☐ Water Pressure: _____
  Hot Water: ☐ Yes   ☐ No
  Cold Water: ☐ Yes   ☐ No

☐ Sink(s) Drains Correctly
  Leaks: ☐ Yes   ☐ No
  Location of Leaks: _____

☐ Number of Sink(s): _____
  Cracks in Sink(s): ☐ Yes   ☐ No

☐ Sink(s) Faucet
  Sprayer Works: ☐ Yes   ☐ No
  Problems:_____

☐ Sink Trap
  Type: _____
  Problems: _____

☐ Garbage Disposal
  Works Correctly: ☐ Yes   ☐ No
  Problems: _____

Countertops

☐ Type: _____
☐ Stains: ☐ Yes   ☐ No
☐ Cracks: ☐ Yes   ☐ No
☐ Space Between Counter & Sink: ☐ Yes   ☐ No
☐ Rotted Wood: ☐ Yes   ☐ No

Cabinets

☐ Condition:
 Exterior: ☐ Good ☐ Bad
 Interior: ☐ Good ☐ Bad

☐ Number of Cabinets: _____

Electrical System

☐ Number of Electrical Outlets: _____
 Types of Outlets: _____
 Problems: _____

☐ Electrical Circuits: _____

☐ Lighting: _____
 Problems: _____

Additional Notes

_____

_____

_____

_____

_____

_____

_____

_____

CHECKLIST THREE: THE BATHROOM

Tub / Shower

☐ Exhaust Fan
Problems: _____

Exhaust Fan Discharge: ☐ Side of House ☐ Through Roof

☐ Moisture Damage
☐ Yes ☐ No

☐ Faucet & Handle Sealed
☐ Yes ☐ No

☐ Tub Properly Caulked & Sealed
☐ Yes ☐ No

☐ Signs of Water Damage / Rotting
☐ Yes ☐ No

Toilet

☐ Condition:
☐ Good ☐ Bad
Area Around Toilet: ☐ Good ☐ Bad

☐ Toilet Tank:
☐ Good ☐ Bad

Sink

☐ Sink Condition:
☐ Good ☐ Bad

☐ Type of Trap: ☐ S-Trap ☐ P-Trap
☐ Good ☐ Bad
Problems: _____

☐ Faucet / Handle Condition:
  ☐ Good   ☐ Bad

Electrical System

☐ Number of Electrical Outlets: _____

☐ GFCI: ☐ Yes   ☐ No

Additional Notes

_____

_____

_____

_____

_____

_____

_____

_____

CHECKLIST FOUR A: THE BASEMENT

Appearance

☐ Finished
   ☐ Yes   ☐ No

Structural

☐ Overall Condition (check entire basement):
   ☐ Good   ☐ Bad

☐ Condition of Joints:
   ☐ Good   ☐ Bad

☐ Condition of Stairs:
   ☐ Good   ☐ Bad

Walls

☐ Signs of Water Damage:
   ☐ Yes   ☐ No
Sources of Water Damage: _____
_____

Floor

☐ Cracks:
   ☐ Yes   ☐ No

☐ Signs of Pipe Leakage:
   ☐ Yes   ☐ No

☐ Source Pump:
   ☐ Yes   ☐ No
Type: _____

Floor Drains

☐ Floor Drain Present:
  ☐ Yes   ☐ No
  Does It Work: ☐ Yes   ☐ No
  Empties To: _____

Lighting

☐ Sufficient Lighting:
  ☐ Yes   ☐ No

☐ Type of Lighting: _____

Additional Notes

_____

_____

_____

_____

_____

_____

_____

_____

CHECKLIST FOUR B: THE CRAWL SPACE

Appearance

☐ Amount of Space: _____

☐ Amount of Moisture: _____

☐ Plastic Covering:
   ☐ Yes   ☐ No

☐ Vented:
   ☐ Yes   ☐ No

☐ Problems with supports, joints, etc.
   ☐ Yes   ☐ No

Additional Notes

_____

_____

_____

_____

_____

_____

_____

_____

CHECKLIST FIVE: ELECTRICAL WIRING

Electrical Service / Capacity

☐ Volts of Electricity Running into House: _____
Sufficient: ☐ Yes ☐ No

☐ Condition of Wires Running from Street into House:
☐ Good ☐ Bad

☐ Condition of Panel Box:
☐ Good ☐ Bad

Panel Box

☐ Location:
☐ Inside ☐ Outside

☐ Condition:
☐ Good ☐ Bad

☐ Type:
☐ Fuses ☐ Circuit Breaker

☐ Panel Cover:
☐ Yes ☐ No

☐ Sufficient Wiring
☐ Good ☐ Bad
Type of Wiring: _____

☐ Potential Problems: _____
_____
_____

Grounding

☐ Location of Grounding Rod: _____

☐ Grounding Rod Properly Connected:
  ☐ Yes   ☐ No

☐ Problems With Grounding Rod: _____
_____

Potential Problems / Violations

☐ Knob and Tube Wiring:
  ☐ Yes   ☐ No

☐ Other Wiring Problems:
  ☐ Yes   ☐ No
  Describe: _____

☐ Outside Wiring Outlets:
  Describe: _____

☐ Inside Wiring Outlets:
  Describe: _____

Additional Notes

_____
_____
_____
_____
_____
_____
_____

CHECKLIST SIX A: PLUMBING

Plumbing

☐ All Equipment Present
    ☐ Yes   ☐ No

☐ Water Flow:
    ☐ Good   ☐ Bad

☐ Supply Piping Problems: _____
_____

☐ Water Supply:
    ☐ Public   ☐ Well
    If Well:
        Type: _____
        Depth: _____

Recently Tested:	☐ Yes	☐ No
Type of Pump: _____		
Pump Condition:	☐ Good	☐ Bad
Storage Tank Condition:	☐ Good	☐ Bad
Pressure Switch:	☐ Yes	☐ No
Pressure Switch Condition:	☐ Good	☐ Bad
Pressure Relief Switch:	☐ Yes	☐ No
Pressure Relief Switch Condition: ☐ Good		☐ Bad

Additional Notes

_____
_____
_____
_____

CHECKLIST SIX B: SEPTIC

Septic

☐ Drainage Pipes:
Types of Pipes: _____
Problems: _____
_____

☐ Supply Pipes
Types of Pipes: _____
Problems: _____
_____

☐ Shut-Off Valve:
☐ Yes ☐ No

Additional Notes

_____
_____
_____
_____

CHECKLIST SEVEN: THE ATTIC

The Attic

☐ Entrance Point: _____

☐ Type of Attic: _____

☐ Insulation: _____
   Problems: _____

☐ Vents / Ventilation: _____
   Kitchen: _____
   Bathroom: _____
   Problems: _____

☐ Supply Pipes
   Types of Pipes: _____
   Problems: _____

☐ Shut-Off Valve:
   ☐ Yes   ☐ No

Roof Cracks / Leaks

☐ Signs of Leaking:
   ☐ Yes   ☐ No

Fire Hazard

☐ Problems With Chimneys:
   ☐ Yes   ☐ No

Violations

☐ Problems With Wiring / Lighting:
   ☐ Yes   ☐ No

☐ Problems With Vent Stacks / Exhaust:
   ☐ Yes   ☐ No

Additional Points

☐ Equipment Condition:
   ☐ Good   ☐ Bad

☐ Attic Fan:
   ☐ Yes   ☐ No

☐ Structure Above Attic:
   ☐ Yes   ☐ No

Additional Notes

_____

_____

_____

_____

CHECKLIST EIGHT A: HEATING

Heating

- Type of Heating: _____

- Age of Furnace / Boiler: _____
  Condition: ☐ Good   ☐ Bad

- Fire Places: _____
  Condition: ☐ Good   ☐ Bad

Additional Notes

_____

_____

_____

CHECKLIST EIGHT B

Heated Air Systems

- Type: _____

- Thermostat: _____
  Condition: ☐ Good   ☐ Bad

- Ducts: _____
  Condition: ☐ Good   ☐ Bad

Additional Notes

_____

_____

_____

CHECKLIST EIGHT C

Hot Water Systems

☐ Type: _____

☐ Thermostat: _____
   Condition: ☐ Good   ☐ Bad

☐ Pipes: _____
   Condition: ☐ Good   ☐ Bad

☐ Temperature / Pressure Gauge: _____
   Condition: ☐ Good   ☐ Bad

Additional Notes

_____

_____

_____

CHECKLIST EIGHT D

Steam Heating Systems

☐ Type: _____

☐ Thermostat: _____
   Condition: ☐ Good   ☐ Bad

☐ Pipes: _____
   Condensation Return Line: ☐ Good   ☐ Bad

Additional Notes

_____

_____

_____

CHECKLIST EIGHT E

Oil Burners

☐ Overall Condition:
   ☐ Good   ☐ Bad

☐ Look / Smell / Listen (comments & findings):
_____
_____

☐ Additional Checks:
_____

Additional Notes

_____
_____
_____

CHECKLIST EIGHT F

Electric Heating

☐ Type: _____
   Condition: ☐ Good   ☐ Bad

☐ Thermostat Type: _____
   Condition: ☐ Good   ☐ Bad

☐ Baseboard Heaters:
   ☐ Yes   ☐ No

☐ Location of Electrical Outlets: _____

Additional Notes

_____

_____

_____

CHECKLIST EIGHT G

Wood Stove

☐ Condition:
    ☐ Good   ☐ Bad

☐ Area Around Stove: _____
    Condition: ☐ Good   ☐ Bad

☐ Flue Pipe: _____
    Condition: ☐ Good   ☐ Bad

☐ Catalytic Converter:
    ☐ Yes   ☐ No

Additional Notes

_____

_____

_____

CHECKLIST EIGHT H

Fireplace

☐ Condition of Fireplace:
    ☐ Good   ☐ Bad

☐ Condition of Masonry Around Fireplace:
☐ Good ☐ Bad

☐ Condition of Chimney:
☐ Good ☐ Bad

☐ Gas Fireplace:
☐ Yes ☐ No
Type: _____
Condition: ☐ Good ☐ Bad

Additional Notes

_____
_____
_____

CHECKLIST EIGHT I

Cooling

☐ Rating (BTUs): _____

☐ Type: _____
Condition: ☐ Good ☐ Bad

☐ Sufficient Size:
☐ Yes ☐ No

Additional Notes

_____
_____
_____

CHECKLIST NINE: APPLIANCE/ UTILITY ROOM

Appliances / Utility Room

Fixed Appliances

Type   Condition / Problem:

1.) _____   _____

                                     _____

2.) _____   _____

                                     _____

3.) _____   _____

                                     _____

4.) _____   _____

                                     _____

Moveable Appliances

☐ Clothes Washer:
   ☐ Yes   ☐ No
   Condition
   ☐ Good   ☐ Bad

☐ Clothes Dryer:
   ☐ Yes   ☐ No
   Condition
   ☐ Good   ☐ Bad

☐ Other Appliances:
   ☐ Yes   ☐ No
   Condition
   ☐ Good   ☐ Bad

CHECKLIST TEN: EXTERIOR DOORS

Exterior Doors

Type / Location

Condition / Problem:

1.) _____   _____

     _____

2.) _____   _____

     _____

3.) _____   _____

     _____

4.) _____   _____

     _____

Additional Notes

_____

_____

_____

CHECKLIST ELEVEN: SIDING

Siding

☐   Type of Siding: _____

Condition: ☐   Good   ☐   Bad

Problems:

☐   Yes   ☐   No

Additional Notes

_____

_____

_____

CHECKLIST TWELVE A: FOUNDATIONS

Foundations

☐ Supports for the House
    ☐ Footers   ☐ Piers   ☐ Columns   ☐ Pilasters
    Condition: ☐ Good   ☐ Bad
    Problems:
    ☐ Yes   ☐ No

☐ Type of Foundation: _____
    Problems:
    ☐ Rotting   ☐ Cracked   ☐ Too Low   ☐ Other

Additional Notes

_____

_____

_____

CHECKLIST TWELVE B: DECKS

Decks

☐ Approximate Age of Deck: _____
    Condition: ☐ Good   ☐ Bad

☐ Problems with Deck Surface:
    ☐ Yes   ☐ No

☐ Problems with Deck Railing:
    ☐ Yes   ☐ No

☐ Problems with Support Posts:
    ☐ Yes   ☐ No

Additional Notes

_____

_____

_____

CHECKLIST THIRTEEN: THE GARAGE

The Garage

- ☐ Type of Garage
  - ☐ Attached ☐ Detached

- ☐ Exterior:
  Siding Condition:
  - ☐ Good   ☐ Bad   ☐ n/a

  Window / Door Condition:
  - ☐ Good   ☐ Bad   ☐ n/a

  Roof / Gutter Condition:
  - ☐ Good   ☐ Bad   ☐ n/a

- ☐ Interior:
  Garage Door Condition:
  - ☐ Good   ☐ Bad   ☐ n/a

  Roof Condition:
  - ☐ Good   ☐ Bad   ☐ n/a

  Floor Condition:
  - ☐ Good   ☐ Bad   ☐ n/a

- ☐ Heater:
  - ☐ Yes   ☐ No

- ☐ Electricity:
  - ☐ Yes   ☐ No

Additional Notes

_____

_____

_____

CHECKLIST FOURTEEN: THE ROOF

The Roof

☐ Type of Garage: _____

☐ Overall Appearance:
   ☐ Good   ☐ Bad
   Problems:
   ☐ Yes   ☐ No

☐ Gutters:
   Type: _____
   Condition:
   ☐ Good   ☐ Bad
   Downspouts:
   Condition:
   ☐ Good   ☐ Bad

Additional Notes

_____

_____

_____

CHECKLIST FIFTEEN A: DRIVEWAYS

Driveways

☐ Type: _____
  Width: _____

☐ Sloped:
  ☐ Yes   ☐ No
  Potential Problems: _____

☐ Overall Condition:
  ☐ Good   ☐ Bad

Additional Notes

_____

_____

_____

CHECKLIST FIFTEEN B: WALKWAYS

Walkways / Sidewalks / Patios

☐ Walkways / Sidewalks:
  ☐ Yes   ☐ No
  Condition:
  ☐ Good   ☐ Bad

☐ Patio(s):
  ☐ Yes   ☐ No
  Condition:
  ☐ Good   ☐ Bad

Additional Notes

_____

_____

_____

CHECKLIST FIFTEEN C: BALCONIES

Balconies

☐ Footers:
Condition:
☐ Good ☐ Bad

☐ Support Posts:
Condition:
☐ Good ☐ Bad

☐ Railing:
Condition:
☐ Good ☐ Bad

☐ Balcony Surface:
Condition:
☐ Good ☐ Bad

Additional Notes

_____

_____

_____

CHECKLIST FIFTEEN D: LAWN

Lawn

☐ Signs of Flooding:
   ☐ Yes   ☐ No

☐ Unhealthy Lawn:
   ☐ Yes   ☐ No

☐ Shrubs:
   ☐ Yes   ☐ No

☐ Trees:
   ☐ Yes   ☐ No

☐ Fences:
   ☐ Yes   ☐ No

Additional Notes

_____

_____

_____

CHECKLIST FIFTEEN E: POOL

Swimming Pool

☐ Type of Pool: _____

☐ Age: _____

☐ Certificate:
   ☐ Yes   ☐ No

☐ Amount of Water Lost Per Day: _____

☐ Signs of Leaking:
    ☐ Yes   ☐ No

☐ Problems Outside Pool:
    ☐ Yes   ☐ No

☐ Problems Inside Pool:
    ☐ Yes   ☐ No

Additional Notes

_____

_____

_____

CHECKLIST FIFTEEN F: OTHER

Other Buildings

Type / Location	Condition / Problem:
1.) _____	_____
	_____
2.) _____	_____
	_____

Additional Notes

_____

_____

_____

CHECKLIST SIXTEEN

Areas of Concern

☐ Asbestos:
  ☐ Yes   ☐ No

☐ Lead Poisoning:
  ☐ Yes   ☐ No

☐ Radon Testing:
  ☐ Yes   ☐ No

☐ Carbon Monoxide Testing:
  ☐ Yes   ☐ No

☐ Termites and Other Infestations:
  ☐ Yes   ☐ No

☐ Fuel Tanks:
  ☐ Yes   ☐ No

☐ Water Quality:
  ☐ Good   ☐ Bad

Additional Notes

_____

_____

_____

FORM 1: SETTING OF INSPECTION

Setting of Inspection

Address of Inspection: _____

_____

_____

Inspected By: _____

Date: _____

Time Inspection Began: _____

People Present During Inspection: _____

_____

_____

_____

Special Circumstances / Occurrences: _____

_____

_____

_____

_____

_____

_____

_____

_____

_____

_____

_____

Time of Completion: _____

FORM 2: QUESTIONS FOR SELLER / OWNER

Questions for Seller / Owner

1.) _____
_____
_____
_____

2.) _____
_____
_____
_____

3.) _____
_____
_____
_____

4.) _____
_____
_____
_____

5.) _____
_____
_____
_____

6.) _____
_____
_____
_____

FORM 3: QUESTIONS FOR A PROFESSIONAL

Questions for a Professional

1.) _____

_____

_____

_____

2.) _____

_____

_____

_____

3.) _____

_____

_____

_____

4.) _____

_____

_____

_____

5.) _____

_____

_____

_____

6.) _____

_____

_____

_____

SIMPLE CHECKLIST

Home Interior	Poor	Average	Excellent
Bedrooms			
Bathrooms			
Floor Plan			
Closet Space			
Fireplace/Stove			
Cable/Satellite			
Living Room			
Dining Room			
Den/Study			
Media Room			
Kitchen			
Laundry Room			
Walls and Ceilings			
Carpets and Floors			
Basements/Attics			
Garage			
Bonus/Storage			

Home Interior	Poor	Average	Excellent
Plumbing			
Electrical			
Insulation			
Heating/Cooling			
Paint/Stain			
Sound Barriers			
Overall Interior			
Home's Exterior			
Fencing			
Yard Area			
Gutters			
Roofing			
Patio/Deck			
Screened Porch			
Siding			
Windows			
Landscaping			
General Curb Appeal			

Home Interior	Poor	Average	Excellent
Garden			
Crawl space			
Foundation			
Driveway			
Sidewalk			
Paint/Stain			
Overall Exterior			

APPENDIX B

MOST IMPORTANT DEFECTS IN ANY HOME

Familiarize yourself with the following list before you go home shopping so that you do not buy trouble. Eliminating problems before they start is smart and avoiding buying a home with a potential major problem is smarter. If a home inspector's report consists of check lists void of needed detail, checking off good, fair poor, adequate, inadequate, you should inquire about remedies and their costs.

COMMON HOUSE DEFECTS	
EXTERIOR	You should be sure that the land around the home is properly graded to divert water away from the home. Roof wear may be apparent if the wear is advanced, but a roof that is starting to age is a more subtle defect that you may wish to have a professional inspect. Resurfacing a roof costs thousands of dollars and will cost much more if the existing roofing needs to be removed before re-roofing. If a roof needs to be resurfaced in the foreseeable future, this may be a negotiable item. Similarly, the siding of the house should be carefully inspected because re-siding a house can also cost thousand of dollars. Likewise, replacement of old defective windows can cost thousands.

COMMON HOUSE DEFECTS

INTERIOR	Basement areas of the home should be checked for signs of water intrusion, such as water stains, mildew, damp, efflorescence on the walls and floors, and damaged floors. Also look for water proofing systems and a sump pump. They can help reduce the risk of flooding in the basement but may not be able to eliminate water intrusion under all conditions. The cost can be prohibitive if a house needs to have outside water flow redirected.

Inadequate ventilation in an attic can result in accelerated deterioration of the structural roof deck, a major expense involving removing and replacing the roofing shingles and roof deck, and in extreme cases, the roof rafters. This is one defect that should not be overlooked.

Painted surfaces on homes constructed prior to 1978 may contain lead paint which can be a problem if there is widespread deterioration of the paint surface. If you are planning renovation of walls after you move in, lead paint is an issue to consider because its removal must follow federal guidelines to control the spread of lead dust. |
| STRUCTURAL | Bulges, deflects, and irregularities in the roof framing, exterior wall framing, and interior framing, or cracks in the foundation wall indicate a serious structural problem that may be the result of poor design, poor construction techniques, improper structural alteration, water damage, or termite damage. Jacking up a house to replace damaged structural components, or underpinning a defective foundation wall is a major expense. |

COMMON HOUSE DEFECTS

ELECTRICAL	The electrical system should be checked by a professional. Once the wiring is exposed, be sure that the home inspector looks for problems in the panel such as burned wiring, over-fused circuits (the fuse or circuit breaker is too large for the wire size), improper wiring connections, openings in the panel (where a child can put a finger into the panel!), or homeowner-installed wiring. In addition to checking for an adequate number of electrical switches and convenience outlets in the house, the outlets should be checked for open ground and wiring reversal conditions. Throughout the house, dead ended wiring and exposed wiring should be on the list of defects you want to check. Homes wired in the mid '60s to mid '70s may have aluminum wiring and, if so, a professional should determine if an approved retrofit has been installed at the wiring connections; if not, a potential fire safety hazard exists. If the home is very old, it may have knob and tube wiring, which is ancient and hazardous. Extensive wiring replacement to meet current codes can cost thousands of dollars.
PLUMBING	Be wary of old lead and galvanized steel water supply pipes: replacement costs thousands. Have a professional check the piping distribution in the house for deterioration, incompatible piping materials, and leaks. Your engineer should carry a moisture meter to evaluate any suspect plaster or wall board on the ceilings and walls caused by water leaks; replacing the piping network in the walls and ceilings is a major expense. Be sure to check all the fixtures and faucets for proper operation and also check tiled bathtub and shower enclosures for integrity.

COMMON HOUSE DEFECTS

HEATING & AIR CONDITIONING	Look for defective furnace heat exchangers. This type of problem is not always easy to uncover and usually means that the furnace will require replacement at an expense of $3,000 to $4,000. Boilers that are starting to leak will also require replacement and a typical cost is $3,000 to $5,000. Make sure that the heat distribution is satisfactory and that the heat distribution piping or duct work is in good condition. A professional should check safety concerns, such as defective controls, inoperative emergency switches, evidence of past malfunctions, and carbon monoxide emissions. Be careful of special problems associated with radiant floor heating and other less common systems. Have any underground oil storage tanks tested for integrity; they can cause thousands of dollars in environmental damage. Another environmental concern is the existence of insulation that may contain asbestos and is especially hazardous if the material is friable. The engineer should advise you to have any suspect material laboratory tested. Test the central air-conditioning system to be sure that it is cooling properly; replacement of an air-conditioning compressor can cost $2,000 to $5,000.
DEFERRED MAINTENANCE	Be very careful of homes where no maintenance has been done; if a home has been poorly maintained and there are obvious problems, proceed with extreme caution. A "handyman's special" is best acquired by a handy man. Be careful of homes where there is obvious plumbing and electrical work, as well as structural additions and renovations that were not professionally installed and were most likely installed by the home owner; correcting these defects can cost thousands of dollars. You should never pay for work that the seller did not want to pay for.

APPENDIX C

HOME INSPECTION CHECKLIST TWO

ADDRESS: _____

_____

_____

ASKING PRICE:: _____

BID PRICE (MY OFFER): _____

SCHOOL DISTRICT: _____

YEAR BUILT: _____ HOUSE STYLE: _____

NO. OF BEDROOMS: _____ NO. OF BATHROOMS: _____ SQ. FT: _____

AMENITIES: _____

REAL ESTATE AGENT'S NAME: _____

REAL ESTATE AGENT'S TELEPHONE NO.: _____ FAX NO.: _____

E-MAIL: _____

DATE: _____

COMMENTS: _____

_____

_____

HOME INSPECTION CHECKLIST TWO

EXTERIOR:

LAND GRADING:
- ☐ EXCELLENT
- ☐ GOOD
- ☐ FAIR
- ☐ POOR

LANDSCAPING:
- ☐ EXCELLENT
- ☐ GOOD
- ☐ FAIR
- ☐ POOR

PRIVACY:
- ☐ EXCELLENT
- ☐ GOOD
- ☐ FAIR
- ☐ POOR

DRIVEWAY:
- ☐ EXCELLENT
- ☐ GOOD
- ☐ FAIR
- ☐ POOR

WALKWAYS:
- ☐ EXCELLENT
- ☐ GOOD
- ☐ FAIR
- ☐ POOR

GARAGE:
- ☐ EXCELLENT
- ☐ GOOD
- ☐ FAIR
- ☐ POOR
- ☐ ATTACHED
- ☐ DETACHED
- ☐ NO. OF CARS

DECKS:
- ☐ EXCELLENT
- ☐ GOOD
- ☐ FAIR
- ☐ POOR

PATIOS:
- ☐ EXCELLENT
- ☐ GOOD
- ☐ FAIR
- ☐ POOR

PORCHES:
- ☐ EXCELLENT
- ☐ GOOD
- ☐ FAIR
- ☐ POOR

RETAINING WALLS:
- ☐ EXCELLENT
- ☐ GOOD
- ☐ FAIR
- ☐ POOR
- ☐ MASONRY
- ☐ RAILROAD TIES

CHIMNEY:
- ☐ EXCELLENT
- ☐ GOOD
- ☐ FAIR
- ☐ POOR

HOME INSPECTION CHECKLIST TWO

ROOF:
- ☐ EXCELLENT   ☐ GOOD   ☐ FAIR   ☐ POOR
- ☐ SHINGLES   ☐ SLATE   ☐ TILE   ☐ CEDAR

ROOF LEADERS & GUTTERS:
- ☐ EXCELLENT   ☐ GOOD   ☐ FAIR   ☐ POOR

EXTERIOR FACADES:
- ☐ EXCELLENT   ☐ GOOD   ☐ FAIR   ☐ POOR
- ☐ WOOD SHINGLES ☐ VINYL   ☐ STUCCO ☐ BRICK
- ☐ WOOD SIDING   ☐ ALUMINUM   ☐ STONE
- ☐ ASBESTOS CEMENT SHINGLES

EXTERIOR TRIM:
- ☐ EXCELLENT   ☐ GOOD   ☐ FAIR   ☐ POOR

WINDOWS:
- ☐ EXCELLENT   ☐ GOOD   ☐ FAIR   ☐ POOR
- ☐ SINGLE GLAZED ☐ DOUBLE GLAZED

EXTERIOR DOORS:
- ☐ EXCELLENT   ☐ GOOD   ☐ FAIR   ☐ POOR

COMMENTS: _____

INTERIOR:

CEILINGS:
- ☐ EXCELLENT   ☐ GOOD   ☐ FAIR   ☐ POOR
- ☐ WATER DAMAGE   ☐ PEELING PAINT   ☐ CRACKS
- ☐ NEEDS REPAINTING
- ☐ SHEETROCK   ☐ PLASTER   ☐ TIN   ☐ PANELING
- ☐ ACOUSTIC TILES

HOME INSPECTION CHECKLIST TWO

WALLS:

- ☐ EXCELLENT ☐ GOOD ☐ FAIR ☐ POOR
- ☐ PEELING PAINT ☐ REPAINT ☐ CRACKS
- ☐ REMOVE WALLPAPER
- ☐ SHEETROCK ☐ WALLPAPER ☐ PLASTER ☐ PANELING

FLOORS:

- ☐ EXCELLENT ☐ GOOD ☐ FAIR ☐ POOR
- ☐ UNLEVEL ☐ SQUEAKS ☐ CRACKS
- ☐ EXCELLENT ☐ GOOD ☐ FAIR ☐ POOR
- ☐ CERAMIC TILE ☐ CARPET ☐ SLATE ☐ VINYL
- ☐ MARBLE TILE ☐ OTHER

CLOSETS:

- ☐ EXCELLENT ☐ GOOD ☐ FAIR ☐ POOR
- ☐ ADEQUATE SPACE ☐ INADEQUATE SPACE

DOORS:

- ☐ EXCELLENT ☐ GOOD ☐ FAIR ☐ POOR

WINDOW TREATMENT:

- ☐ EXCELLENT ☐ GOOD ☐ FAIR ☐ POOR

BUILT-IN FURNITURE:

- ☐ EXCELLENT ☐ GOOD ☐ FAIR ☐ POOR

CEILING FIXTURES:

- ☐ EXCELLENT ☐ GOOD ☐ FAIR ☐ POOR

SOURCE OF HEAT IN EACH ROOM:

- ☐ EXCELLENT ☐ GOOD ☐ FAIR ☐ POOR

SOURCE OF AIR-CONDITIONING IN EACH ROOM:

- ☐ EXCELLENT ☐ GOOD ☐ FAIR ☐ POOR

COMMENTS: _____

HOME INSPECTION CHECKLIST TWO

KITCHEN:

GENERAL CONDITION:
- ☐ EXCELLENT ☐ GOOD ☐ FAIR ☐ POOR

APPLIANCES:
- ☐ EXCELLENT ☐ GOOD ☐ FAIR ☐ POOR

CABINETS & COUNTERS:
- ☐ EXCELLENT ☐ GOOD ☐ FAIR ☐ POOR

PANTRY:
- ☐ EXCELLENT ☐ GOOD ☐ FAIR ☐ POOR

COMMENTS: _____

BATHROOM(S):

NUMBER:
- ☐ FULL: _____ ☐ HALF: _____

GENERAL CONDITION:
- ☐ EXCELLENT ☐ GOOD ☐ FAIR ☐ POOR

FIXTURES:
- ☐ EXCELLENT ☐ GOOD ☐ FAIR ☐ POOR

FAUCETS:
- ☐ EXCELLENT ☐ GOOD ☐ FAIR ☐ POOR

CABINETS:
- ☐ EXCELLENT ☐ GOOD ☐ FAIR ☐ POOR

JACUZZI / STEAM SHOWER:
- ☐ EXCELLENT ☐ GOOD ☐ FAIR ☐ POOR

HOME INSPECTION CHECKLIST TWO

WALL TILE:
- ☐ EXCELLENT ☐ GOOD ☐ FAIR ☐ POOR

FIBERGLASS ENCLOSURES:
- ☐ EXCELLENT ☐ GOOD ☐ FAIR ☐ POOR

COMMENTS:_____

LAUNDRY:

GENERAL CONDITION:
- ☐ EXCELLENT ☐ GOOD ☐ FAIR ☐ POOR

COMMENTS: _____

ATTIC:

GENERAL CONDITION:
- ☐ EXCELLENT ☐ GOOD ☐ FAIR ☐ POOR

TYPE:
- ☐ ACCESS VIA HATCH ☐ WALK-UP ☐ ROOM FOR STORAGE

INSULATION:
- ☐ EXCELLENT ☐ GOOD ☐ FAIR ☐ POOR

VENTILATION:
- ☐ EXCELLENT ☐ GOOD ☐ FAIR ☐ POOR

ROOF STRUCTURE:
- ☐ EXCELLENT ☐ GOOD ☐ FAIR ☐ POOR
- ☐ CRACKED ☐ SAGS

COMMENTS: _____

HOME INSPECTION CHECKLIST TWO

BASEMENT:

GENERAL CONDITION:
- ☐ EXCELLENT   ☐ GOOD   ☐ FAIR   ☐ POOR

TYPE:
- ☐ PARTIAL   ☐ CRAWL   ☐ FULL
- ☐ ROOM FOR STORAGE

FOUNDATION WALLS:
- ☐ EXCELLENT   ☐ GOOD   ☐ FAIR   ☐ POOR
- ☐ POURED CONCRETE   ☐ STONE   ☐ BRICK
- ☐ CONCRETE BLOCK   ☐ CRACKS   ☐ BULGES

STRUCTURE:
- ☐ EXCELLENT   ☐ GOOD   ☐ FAIR   ☐ POOR
- ☐ CRACKED   ☐ SAGS   ☐ WATER DAMAGE

SUMP PUMP:
- ☐ EXCELLENT   ☐ GOOD   ☐ FAIR   ☐ POOR

DEHUMIDIFIER:
- ☐ EXCELLENT   ☐ GOOD   ☐ FAIR   ☐ POOR

COMMENTS: _____

ELECTRICAL SYSTEM:

SERVICE TO HOUSE:
- ☐ OVERHEAD   ☐ UNDERGROUND

AMPERAGE:
- ☐ 30   ☐ 60   ☐ 125   ☐ 150   ☐ 200

VOLTAGE:
- ☐ 110   ☐ 110/220   ☐ 110/208/220

HOME INSPECTION CHECKLIST TWO

SERVICE PANEL:
- ☐ BREAKERS ☐ FUSES

ELECTRICAL OUTLETS:
- ☐ EXCELLENT ☐ GOOD ☐ FAIR ☐ POOR
- ☐ 3 PRONG ☐ 2 PRONG

LIGHTING:
- ☐ EXCELLENT ☐ GOOD ☐ FAIR ☐ POOR

COMMENTS: _____

PLUMBING:

GENERAL CONDITION:
- ☐ EXCELLENT ☐ GOOD ☐ FAIR ☐ POOR

SOURCE OF WATER:
- ☐ MUNICIPAL ☐ COMMUNITY ☐ PRIVATE WELL

WATER PRESSURE:
- ☐ EXCELLENT ☐ GOOD ☐ FAIR ☐ POOR

HOT WATER CONDITION:
- ☐ EXCELLENT ☐ GOOD ☐ FAIR ☐ POOR

HOT WATER SOURCE:
- ☐ GAS FIRED ☐ OIL FIRED ☐ SEPARATE TANK
- ☐ ELECTRIC ☐ INTEGRAL WITH SPACE HEATING SYSTEM

WATER PIPE CONDITION:
- ☐ EXCELLENT ☐ GOOD ☐ FAIR ☐ POOR

WATER PIPE MATERIAL:
- ☐ COPPER ☐ BRASS ☐ STEEL ☐ LEAD
- ☐ PLASTIC

HOME INSPECTION CHECKLIST TWO

Drainage, Waste, Vent Pipe Condition:

☐ Excellent ☐ Good ☐ Fair ☐ Poor

Drainage, Waste, Vent Pipe Material:

☐ Copper ☐ Cast-Iron ☐ Steel ☐ Plastic

Sanitary Waste Disposal:

☐ Municipal ☐ Community ☐ Private

Comments: _____

_____

_____

_____

_____

_____

_____

_____

_____

_____

House Inspection Tip #14

Before going to inspect a house, make a list of questions to ask about it. Also, prepare a checklist to make sure that you thoroughly check every detail of the house. Without these lists, you may forget to inspect something vital.

APPENDIX D

Item	What to Inspect	Check
Propane Tank	See if it is securely mounted, and the line is not where people will trip on it. If it is near the driveway, it should have vertical posts or other safety barrier.	
Grading & Drainage	Does the lot slope towards the house, which could cause water to enter? Are there any areas where water builds up and causes issues?	
Landscaping	Are trees too close to lines, chimneys, or roofs? Are there dead trees that need to be removed for safety reasons? Is there any other landscaping needed? Are flower beds keeping water trapped by the house?	
Building Exterior	What condition is the paint in? Are there cracks or crumbly stucco? Any obvious signs of rotting trim? Are the gutters clogged or loose?	
Roof	How long before the shingles will need to be replaced? Are there more than a couple layers of shingles? Is there any sagging in the roof or gaps near chimneys and pipes? Is the trim becoming rotten? Do the soffits sag?	

Item	What to Inspect	Check
Doors	Do they look to be in good shape? Check for mis-alignment as it could mean the walls or foundation is settling.) Are the locks working properly?	
Windows	Are they in good shape? Do you see any glass that is broken or rot near the edges? Are there screens on all windows?	
Foundation	Are there any visible cracks in the foundation? (Over 1/8" or cracks that are mis-aligned are a potential warning sign.) Is the top high enough off the ground so insects cannot easily reach the wood?	
Driveway	Are repairs or resurfacing needed?	
Porches	Are the porch boards solid? Is paint or stain needed? Are the supports sufficient?	
Sheds	Shed doors working? Any light coming in when on the inside?	
Fences	Are the fences in good condition? Are the bases of the fence posts rotting?	
Garage Firewall	Is a firewall (generally this is a 5/8" taped-joint drywall) present between house and garage?	
Garage Floor	Is floor level or cracking badly? Is drain present and in working condition?	
Garage Walls	Are walls in good shape?	
Garage Doors	Garage door working? Are all other doors present working properly?	

Item	What to Inspect	Check
Living Room Walls	Any cracks, bulges, or areas of peeling paint/ wallpaper? Any water stains visible?	
Living Room Ceiling	Any peeling paint visible? Does the ceiling show signs of sagging?	
Living Room Floor	Do you feel any uneven areas on the floor? Any carpeting pulling loose? Do you see any large stains or badly damaged areas?	
Living Room Electrical Outlets	Test all outlets. (Get a handheld tester at a hardware store). Are the outlets working properly and attached firmly to the walls?	
Living Room Windows	Do they open and close with ease? Blinds/ curtains working properly?	
Living Room Lights	Test all light switches.	
Kitchen Walls	Any signs of cracks, bulges, peeling paint, or wallpaper?	
Kitchen Ceiling	Peeling paint visible? Does ceiling show signs of sagging or leak stains?	
Kitchen Floor	Is the floor level or do you se or feel any loose or bulging linoleum? Are the tiles loose? Do you see any large stains or badly damaged areas?	
Kitchen Lights	Test all light switches.	

Item	What to Inspect	Check
Kitchen Electrical Outlets	Are the outlets in working correctly and attached properly to the walls?	
Kitchen Windows	Do they open and close with ease? Blinds/ curtains working properly?	
Kitchen Appliances	Make sure all appliances included in purchase are working properly.	
Kitchen Exhaust Fans	Is the fan working?	
Kitchen Faucets, Sinks, & Drains	Turn on faucets. Watch the color of the water and how long until hot water flows. Does the sink drain easily? Is any moisture present under the sink from a possible leak?	
Bathroom Walls	Any signs of cracks, bulges, peeling paint, or wallpaper?	
Bathroom Ceiling	Peeling paint visible? Does ceiling show signs of sagging or leak stains?	
Bathroom Floor	Does the floor feel level? Is there any loose or bulging linoleum? Loose flooring tiles? Are there any large stains or damaged areas?	
Bathroom Lights	Test all light switches.	
Bathroom Electrical Outlets	Are the outlets in working correctly and attached properly to the walls?	
Bathroom Windows	Do they open and close with ease? Blinds/ curtains working properly?	
Bathroom Exhaust Fan	Turn on the fan. Is it running properly?	

Item	What to Inspect	Check
Bathtub & Shower	Is shower working? Does water drain properly through tub? Any noticeable damage on walls near tub? Do you see any major mineral stains in the tub?	
Toilet	Flush the toilet. Do the valves behind the toilet drip? Is it still dripping after the tank is full?	
Bathroom Mirrors	Is the laminating coming off the mirror? Does it have any cracking?	
Bathroom Faucets, Sinks, & Drains	Turn on faucets. Watch the color of the water and how long until hot water flows. Does the sink drain easily? Is any moisture present under the sink from a possible leak?	
Attic Insulation	Is there enough insulation? Is it in good shape?	
Attic Wires	Is the wiring up-to-date with no bare wires or insulators?	
Attic Roof	Is there light coming in from anywhere? Do you see any sagging? Are the supports sturdy and are there enough?	
Attic Vents	Check for air vents. Do they look to be screened correctly?	
Attic Pests	Do you see any evidence of animals such as droppings or wood shavings?	
Electrical Mast	Does the electrical connection (the mast) look to be secured to the house? Check for bare ends on wires. If any are present they need to be re-taped.	

Item	What to Inspect	Check
Outside Wires	Do you see any wires touching the house? Is there a drip-loop which will keep the rain from getting into the service panel? Are the lines at least 10 feet above the ground or driveway? Are any lines going to outside lights? Are the lights working properly?	
Breaker Box	Do you see breakers but no fuses? (You may be unable to get insurance if you do not have fuses). Are the breakers labeled and the correct sizes (no 30 amp breakers with 20 amp wires)? Is the box covered properly? Check for corroded terminals.	
Wiring	Does the wiring look correct? Are there copper and aluminum wires mixed? Are any splices exposed? Do wires show any signs of burning? Is wiring exposed? Any wire ends exposed which need to be capped? Check to be sure the wiring in the garage is seven feet above the floor.	
Outlets	Make sure all covers are undamaged and have weather protection.	
Basement Water	Do you see any standing water or signs of past water damage?	
Basement Floor Joists	Are floor beams in good shape without sagging, rotting, or insect damage?	
Basement Walls	Do you see any cracks or bulges in the walls?	

Item	What to Inspect	Check
Basement Supports	Do the supports look good? Are any of the supports new? If so, ask the seller why.	
Basement Faucets, Sinks, & Drains	Check faucets and drains.	
Basement Sump Pump	Is it working?	
Basement Floor	Do you see any major cracks on the floor?	
Fireplace Damper	Make sure the damper opens and closes with ease.	
Fireplace Structure	Check for cracks or spaces and make sure a spark-arrester screen is present.	
Chimney	Is it in good shape? Are any bricks separating or beginning to crumble? Check that chimney is firmly attached to house and not pulling away. Do you see any build-up of creosote?	
House Entryway	Is there enough lighting in the entry? Do you see any damage to the floors?	
Furnace	Is the furnace working? (Adjust it to get it to turn on.) Does the fan sound good when on? Is the flame blue (best to be blue) or yellow (yellow is the problem)? Are the ducts attached tightly? Is there any gas smell?	

Item	What to Inspect	Check
Water Heater	Does the hot water get hot? Is the water heater in good working order? Do you see any stains that could be evidence of leaking? Is there any rust on the fittings? Is there a shut-off valve for the water?	
Crawl Space	Can you crawl through the crawl space or is it too small? Can you see any water when you look into the space? Are any of the floorboards sagging or can any damage be seen?	
Stairways	Are the stairs safe? Are there any loose steps or broken edges?	
Air Conditioning	Turn on the air conditioner and make sure it works. Are there any stains or damage that could have been caused by draining?	

AUTHOR BIOGRAPHY & DEDICATION

"To Carrie, Phoebe, and Ellie"

Charles A. Rose was born and raised in upstate New York. He attended Le Moyne College in Syracuse, New York where he received a Bachelor's Degree in English. Charles has been writing for over twenty years. He is currently a teacher in New York where he lives with his wife and children.

GLOSSARY

A

A/C The common abbreviation for air conditioning.

A/C CIRCUIT An alternating current, in which the current flows in one direction and then reverses itself. This type of circuit provides superior flexibility in voltage selection.

ACCELERATOR A chemical used to speed up the time it takes for stucco, plaster, or mortar to set.

ACCESS PANEL A removable panel that allows access to a fixture's plumbing or electrical system; usually located in the wall or the ceiling.

ACCESSIBILITY The ease and convenience of entering a property by tenants, owners, customers, or any other users. Typically refers to foot traffic or automobile traffic, but could also refer to airplane traffic in subdivisions with accompanying landing strip for owners. A lack of accessibility typically results in a lower property value.

ACRE The standard of measurement for property. An acre is calculated in square feet or square yards. One acre equals 4,840 square yards, or 43,560 square feet.

ACRYLIC A clear plastic used to shape the surface of fiberglass bathtubs, whirlpools, shower bases, and shower stalls.

AERATOR A device attached to the end of a faucet which mixes air and water, allowing for a smooth flow.

AGGREGATE The mineral materials, such as crushed stone, slag, water-worn gravel, crushed lava rock, marble chips, and sand, used in roof construction.

AIR CHAMBER An extra piece of pipe installed above the water line and used to absorb pressure when water is turned off at a faucet.

AIR DUCT A means of transporting cooled or heated air.

AIR FILTERS A device used to remove particles of lint and dust from the air. These filters are capable of removing 90% of the dirt if they are not clogged.

AIR INFILTRATION The air that escapes from a building through cracks in the walls, windows, and doors.

AIR SPACE The gap between insulation and the exterior wall which allows moisture to pass through and the wall to dry.

AIRWAY The space between the insulation and the roof boards which allows air to circulate.

AMPACITY The amount of current a wire can carry.

AMPERAGE The rate at which electricity flows through a wire; measured in amperes.

AMPS (AMPERES) The rate of flow of electricity through a conductor.

ANTI-SCALD A special valve that controls the flow of water to prevent burn injuries.

ANTI-SIPHON An apparatus that stops waste water from being reused.

APPRAISAL The estimate of the value of a property on a particular date given by a professional appraiser, usually presented in a written document.

AREA WELLS Barriers around a basement window that restrain the earth.

ASBESTOS A mineral once used in insulation and other materials that can cause respiratory diseases.

ASPHALT PLASTIC CEMENT A material used to bind roofing substances.

ATTIC VENTILATORS A screen opening that is placed in the ceiling of a home which allows air to circulate in the attic.

AWNING WINDOW A window hinged along the top edge which allows it to open outward.

B

BACK NAILING A method of preventing roofing felts from slipping whereby the felts are nailed to the deck under the overlap.

BACKFILL Replacement or excavated dirt into a hole or against a structure.

BACKFLOW The flow of water in any unintended direction.

BACKFLOW PREVENTER An apparatus which stops backflow from entering the water supply.

BACKHAND A type of molding used as a decorative feature.

BACKSPLASH The area above and behind a sink or lavatory which protects the wall from water damage

BALANCING DAMPER A device used to control the amount of air that enters an area.

BARREL ROOF A roof design that is arched in cross sections.

BASE MOLDING Molding that is installed on the top of the baseboard.

BASEBOARD Trim installed where the wall and the floor meet.

BASEBOARD HEAT A heating system in which the unit is found where the baseboard is normally located.

BAY WINDOW A window that

curves outward from the house.

BEDROCK A solid rock layer covered by soil that is strong enough to support a structure.

BELOW GRADE Any part of a building that is located below ground level.

BIFOLD DOOR A door made of panels that are hinged in the middle, allowing them to open in a smaller area than standard doors.

BIPASS DOORS Doors commonly used as closets that slide by each other.

BLIND NAILING A method of nailing in which the heads cannot be seen.

BLISTER A raised spot on a surface which is normally caused by the expansion trapped air, water vapor, or moisture.

BOW The distortion, such as curving, bending, or warping, of a piece of glass or wood.

BRANCH CIRCUIT A type of wiring that travels from a service panel to an outlet. These circuits are protected by fuses and breakers.

BREEZEWAY A covered, open-sided passage that connects two structures

BTU The unit used to measure the quantity of heat.

Buckling – The warping or bending of a material due to wear and tear or water contact.

BUILT-UP ROOF A roof made up of three to five layers of asphalt felt laminated with coal tar, pitch, or asphalt.

BUTTERFLY ROOF A method of roof assembly in which two gables form a dip in the middle.

C

CAMBER A slightly curved surface

CANOPY A roof that overhangs the building

CAP SHEET The top layer in a built up roof.

CASEMENT WINDOW A window with hinges on its sides allowing it to open vertically.

CASING The molding that is used to trim door and window openings

CATCH BASIN A drain located in a low or wet spot that has a pipe on the side and a sediment-collecting pit on the bottom.

CENTERSET A style of bathroom faucet with combined spout and handles with the handles being four inches apart, measured center to center.

CHAIR RAIL A type of molding that is located horizontally on a wall about three feet from the ground.

CHASE A shielded, vertical shaft around a flue pipe or channel in a wall or a ceiling that allows something to pass through.

CHECKRAILS Thick meeting rails that fill the gap between the top and bottom sash of a window.

CIRCUIT An electrical device that begins at a panel box and provides a path for electricity to follow to outlets

CIRCUIT BREAKER A protective switch that opens an electrical circuit when a short occurs.

CLASS "A" FIRE RESISTANCE The highest fire-resistance rating a roof can receive; denotes that roofing can withstand severe exposure to a fire that started outside the building.

CLASS "B" FIRE RESISTANCE Denotes that roofing can withstand moderate exposure from fire originating from outside sources.

CLASS "C" FIRE RESISTANCE Denotes that roofing material can withstand light exposure to a fire that started outside the building.

CLASS B DOOR The classification, according to the Underwriters Laboratories, for a door with a one to one and a half hour rating.

COMBINATION DOOR OR WINDOWS Doors or windows that include removable glass and screen inserts so they provide both winter insulation and summer protection.

CONCEALED NAIL METHOD A method of roofing in which the nails are covered by an overlapping course, keeping them protected from the elements.

CONTINUITY TESTER A tool used to determine if a circuit is open or closed.

CORNERITE Wire mesh cut in strips and bent in a right angle that is used in the corners of walls and ceilings to keep the plaster from cracking.

COVE MOLDING A type concave-faced molding used as trim or to finish interior corners.

COVERAGE The amount of protection the roofing material provides from the weather.

CRAZING A network of cracks on the surface of weathered materials.

CRICKET An elevated construction on the back of a chimney which prevents the accumulation of snow and ice and deflects water

CUPOLA A dome-shaped structure on top of a larger roof.

CUPPING A type of warping in which the edges curl.

CURTAIN DRAIN A structure which serves to redirect storm and drain water away from a building.

CUTOFF VALVES Valves usually located under sinks that shut water off without cutting the water off throughout the entire house.

D

DAMPPROOFING Treatment used on concrete, brick, or stone surfaces to resist water, especially the absorption of rain water.

DECAY The destruction and disintegration of wood due to the action of fungi.

DESIGN PRESSURE The amount of pressure a product can withstand.

DIRECT GAIN SYSTEM A solar heating system in which sunlight directly warms the interior of a building.

DIRECT NAILING Nailing that is done perpendicular to a surface.

DIVERTER A type of valve commonly used in showers, tubs, bidets, and sinks that directs water to various outlets.

DORMER A window places vertically in a sloping roof.

DOUBLE HUNG WINDOW A type of window that can be opened from the top and the bottom due to vertically sliding sashes.

DRIP CAP A molding placed on the top of a door or window frame which causes water to drip outside the frame.

DRIP EDGE A projection designed to allow water to drip away from a building.

DRY-IN The process of waterproofing a building.

DUCT A tube or passage that moves and distributes air.

DWV (DRAINAGE, WASTE, AND VENT) The system of pipes that removes waste water.

E

EASEMENT The right given to a non-ownership party to use a certain part of the property for specified purposes, such as servicing power lines or cable lines.

EAVE The lower edge of a roof that projects beyond the side wall.

EGRESS A term for a way to exit a home. An egress window is required in every bedroom and basement.

ELBOW An extension of a downspout that alters the direction of the water.

ELEVATION The vertical side of a building.

EMULSION A mixture of asphalt and fillers in water used as a roof coating.

ENERGY EFFICIENCY RATIO An air conditioning performance rating based on the number of BTUs that are delivered per watt of power consumed.

ESCUTCHEON A decorative piece that conceals the faucet stem and the hole in the fixture or wall.

EXHAUST FAN A fan that moves air from the inside of a structure.

EXPOSED NAIL METHOD A method of nailing in which the nails are exposed to the elements because they are driven into the overlapping course of the roof.

EXPOSURE The part of the roof that is exposed to the elements after it is installed.

EXPOSURE I GRADE PLYWOOD The only type of plywood the American Plywood Association approves for exterior use.

F

FAÇADE The front of a building or a false front.

FACE BRICK A type of brick made specifically for outside use

FALL/FLOW The angle or slope of a pipe that allows for drainage.

FASTENERS Hardware such as screws and nails used to secure parts of a building.

FELT A material combined with asphalt that is installed as a secondary layer of roofing to increase protection.

FEMALE IPS A pipe connection in which the fittings are found on the inside.

FENESTRATION Windows or panels of glass located on the outside of a building.

FERRUL The metal tubes that keep gutters open.

FIBERED ALUMINUM ROOF COATING A reflective barrier used on roofs, metal surfaces, and brickwork that helps to reflect the sun's rays, thereby reducing energy costs.

FIELD MEASURE The process of taking measurements in the home rather than relying on the blueprints.

FINISH A term used in hardware to describe any metal fastenings left exposed on cabinets.

FINISH CARPENTRY The final carpentry done in a home, such as hanging interior doors.

FIRE STOP An object or surface used to stop the spread of fire and smoke through the space itself.

FIRE WALL A wall built to stop the spread of fire.

FLAGSTONE A large, flat stone used in walkways and patios.

FLASH POINT The temperature at which a material will catch fire.

FLAT PAINT A type of paint used in the interior of homes that has little or no sheen.

FLATWORK A term used to refer to concrete floors, driveways, basements, and sidewalks.

FLOOR PLAN The layout of a building.

FLOW RATE The rate at which water flows from an outlet.

FLUE A vent that allows smoke, gas, or air to escape.

FORCED AIR HEATING A type of heating in which natural gas, propane, oil, or electricity is used as a fuel.

FOUNDATION The substructure of a building which supports the structure above it.

FREE-TAB SHINGLES Shingles without any type of self-sealing adhesive device.

G

GABLE The triangular end of an exterior wall formed by two sloping roofs.

GAMBREL ROOF A type of roof which has two slopes.

GAS LATERAL The place in the yard where the gas line service is.

GAUGE The thickness of a material, such as sheet metal or wire.

GLOBE VALVE A valve that adjusts the flow of water to any desirable rate.

GLOSS (PAINT OR ENAMEL) A paint or enamel that has a sheen or luster.

GPF (GALLONS PER FLUSH) The unit that measures the flow rate of toilets.

GPM (GALLONS PER MINUTE) The unit that measures the flow rate of faucets and shower heads.

GRADE MW A grade of brick that will withstand moderate weather and has a moderate resistance to freezing.

GRADE NW A grade of brick that will withstand no weather and is used for interior work.

GRADE SW A grade of brick that will withstand severe weather and has a high resistance to freezing.

GROUND A connection between the earth and an electrical circuit.

GUTTER A channel along the eaves of a roof that collects rain water and allows it to drain.

H

HARDWARE A term used to refer to any metal accessory.

HEAT PUMP A method of heating and cooling that uses compression and decompression.

HEATING LOAD The amount

of heat needed to maintain a specific temperature during the winter.

HIP ROOF A type of roof with four sloping sides.

HOME RUN A wiring method in which the electrical cable transmits power from the main circuit breaker to the first electrical box, plug, or switch in the circuit.

HVAC An acronym for heating, ventilation, and air conditioning.

I

ID (INSIDE DIAMETER) A method for sizing pipe in which the diameter of the inside of a pipe is taken.

INSIDE DRAIN A drain on a roof that is located somewhere other than the perimeter which drains water inside the building through closed pipes.

INSULATION A material used to reduce the transfer of heat.

INTERLOCKING SHINGLES Shingles that lock into each other to provide wind resistance.

K

KEYLESS A type of light fixture that has a pull string.

KILOWATT One thousand watts; the unit of measure for electrical consumption.

L

LAMINATED SHINGLES A type of shingle with one than one tab, causing extra thickness.

LEACH FIELD The method used to treat and dispose sewage in rural areas.

LEAN-TO ROOF A roof with a slope that is built against another wall.

LIMIT SWITCH A protective device that turns off a furnace if it gets too hot.

LOOKOUT A bracket that

supports any overhanging portion of a roof.

LOW SLOPE APPLICATION A method of roofing in which the shingles on roof slopes are installed between two and four inches per foot.

M

MAIN VENT The primary vent to which other vents are connected.

MALE IPS A pipe connection in which the fittings are found on the outside.

MASONRY Stone, brick, or other similar materials bonded together with mortar to form a structure.

MASTIC A putty-like material often used as a waterproof compound for exterior walls and roofs.

MELT POINT Temperature at which asphalt turns into a liquid.

MINERAL SURFACED ROOFING Roofing materials with a top layer of granules.

MINISPREAD A type of faucet with separate spout and handles designed to fit four inch center-to-center holes.

MIXING VALVE A valve that adjusts the temperature by mixing hot and cold water before delivery.

MOLDING Decorative trim used to cover doors and window openings.

MULLION A vertical divider between doors or windows that holds together glass and other materials.

N

NATURAL FINISH A finish applied to wood that does not significantly change the natural color or grain.

NESTING A method of re-roofing that involves layering new shingles over old shingles

NON-FIBERED ALUMINUM ROOF COATING A thin, reflective barrier used on roofs to deflect the sun's rays, thereby prolonging the surface's life.

NORMAL SLOPE APPLICATION A method of roofing that involves installing shingles on roof slopes between four and twenty-one inches per foot.

NUCLEAR METER Tool used to detect the presence of moisture.

O

OD (OUTSIDE DIAMETER) A method for sizing pipe in which the diameter of the inside of a pipe is taken.

OVERHANG The part of a roof that hangs over the wall.

P

P TRAP A plumbing device that stops sewer odors from escaping into the house.

PADDING Any kind of material placed under carpet to add a softer feel, isolate sound, and prolong the life of the carpet.

PERIMETER DRAIN The drainage system that is installed below ground around the perimeter of the foundation and redirects water away from the foundation.

PITCH A term used to define the incline and angle of a roof.

PLASTIC ROOF CEMENT A type of waterproofing used in new construction that stops leaks.

PLOT PLAN An overhead view that shows how a building sits on the lot, along with setbacks, easements, rights of way, and drainage.

PONDING The gathering of water on a roof due to poor drainage.

POROSITY The density of a material and its ability to absorb liquids.

POWER RATE The energy rate measured in watts.

PRESERVATIVE A substance applied to wood that helps it resist fungi, insects, and other destructive elements.

R

RADIANT HEATING A method of heating which involves heating the floors, walls, and ceilings.

RAKE EDGE The overhang of a roof plane beyond wall below it.

RECEPTACLE Another term for an electrical outlet.

RESILIENT FLOORING Thin flooring coverings that are able to return to their original shape.

RETURN A vent that sends cold air to be heated.

RISE In stairs, the vertical distance from one step to another.

ROOF SHEATHING Flat boards placed on the roof rafters onto which the roofing material is laid.

ROUGH Hardware that is hidden from view.

S

SANITARY SEWER The drain line used to collect waste water from the bathroom, kitchen, and laundry drains.

SCUPPER An opening for drainage of water from a flat roof.

SEMIGLOSS (PAINT OR ENAMEL) A paint or enamel that has some luster but is not glossy when dry.

SETBACK THERMOSTAT A thermostat that can be programmed for certain temperatures at different times on different days.

SHED ROOF A roof with only one sloping plane.

SHORT CIRCUIT An unwanted situation in which a negative and a positive source come in contact with each other.

SHUTOFF VALVE A valve that stops the water supply to one fixture without affecting other fixtures.

SIDING The outside covering of a building meant to protect the structure from the weather.

SLOPE The degree of a roof's incline.

SMOOTH-SURFACED ROOFING A type of roofing material that is covered with ground talc or mica rather than granules.

STAIN A thin coating used to color wood without concealing the grain or texture.

STATIC VENT A vent without a fan.

STEM ASSEMBLY A valve with a moving part that controls the water's temperature and amount by moving up and down to open and close the valve.

STRAIGHT STOP A stop valve installed on the supply line between the floor and the faucet or toilet.

STUCCO A mixture of sand and cement used as an exterior finish.

SWITCH An apparatus that makes or breaks an electric circuit.

T

TEMPERED Another word for strengthened.

THERMAL INSULATION Any material placed in walls, ceilings, or floors used to reduce heat flow.

TOE-NAILING The method of nailing in which nails are driven in at a slant

TONGUE AND GROOVE A type of flooring in which the tongue of one boards fits into the groove of another board.

TRAP A plumbing device that holds water to stop air, gas, and vermin from getting back into a fixture.

TRIM The finishing materials in a building that frame or edge features around openings, floors, and ceilings.

V

VACUUM BREAKER An anti-siphon device that acts as a backflow preventer.

VARNISH A mixture of drying oil used as a transparent coating.

VOLTAGE A measure of electricity's potential.

W

WARPING A distortion in a material, especially wood.

WASTE PIPE AND VENT The plumbing system that transports waste water to the sewage system.

WATTAGE The electrical unit of power.

WEATHERIZATION Work done on a building's exterior to reduce energy consumption, such as insulation, storm windows, and weather-stripping.

WEATHERSTRIP Pieces of thin metal that prevent air and moisture from seeping in through windows and doors.

INDEX

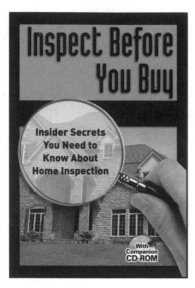

DID YOU BORROW THIS COPY?

Have you been borrowing a copy of *Inspect Before You Buy: Insider Secrets You Need to Know About Home Inspection* from a friend, colleague or library? Wouldn't you like your own copy for quick and easy reference? To order, photocopy the form below and send to:

Atlantic Publishing Company
1405 SW 6th Ave.
Ocala, FL 34471-0640